MARRIAGE AND
PARTNERSHIPS IN THE UK

INCLUDES SAME SEX MARRIAGE AND MIXED SEX CIVIL PARTNERSHIPS

REVISED EDITION
STEVE RICHARDS

Editor: Roger Sproston

Emerald Guides

Emerald Guides

ISBN
978-1-913342-49-4

Printed by 4edge www.4edge.co.uk

Cover design by BW Studios Derby

Contents

Introduction

Covid 19 and the impact on Marriage/Civil Partnerships

PART ONE-CONVENTIONAL MARRIAGE AND DIVORCE IN THE UK

PART TWO-CIVIL PARTNERSHIPS IN THE UK

PART THREE-SAME SEX MARRIAGES IN THE UK

****

Introduction

This revised and extended edition of Marriage and Civil partnerships in the UK, (revised to **2020**) will be invaluable to either the layperson who wishes to know more generally about heterosexual marriage, civil partnerships and same sex marriage, or for the student or professional who wishes to know more about the detail of the law.

The book is structured in such a way that the initial chapters dealing with the respective areas provide a general overview, with the subsequent chapters dealing with the finer detail.

This book covers marriage generally, the Civil Partnerships Act 2004 and the Civil Partnership Regulations (Same Sex Couples) 2019, also The Marriage (Same Sex Couples Act) 2013. Chapters 1 and 2 provides an overview of marriage generally, plus divorce and dissolution, chapter 3 The Civil partnerships Act 2004, whilst chapters 4-9 provide more detailed provisions of the Act. Chapter 10 provides a detailed overview of the 2013 marriage (Same Sex Couples) Act 2013. Also covered is the impact of COVID 19 on marriage ceremonies.

The book will act as an ideal introduction to the law and procedure of marriage and civil partnerships and also same sex partnerships and is suitable for both students, professionals and laypeople who wish to keep up to date with this area.

The Impact of COVID 19 on Weddings and Civil Partnerships generally

On 23 March 2020, the UK Government responded to the unprecedented pandemic sweeping across the world by introducing an equally unprecedented lockdown in England, with the devolved nations of Scotland, Wales and Northern Ireland immediately following suit.

What Are the Latest Rules for Weddings?

The new wedding guidelines, announced on 29th June, implemented a series of rules for weddings. These include social distancing, hand washing before the exchange of rings and avoiding singing.

Here's what the Government advice says:

Ceremonies must be kept "as short as reasonably possible" and limited to the legally binding parts. No more than 30 people may attend, including the couple and staff at the venue. Ceremonies must be in a "COVID-19 secure environment" with guests following the 2 metre rule, or "1 metre plus" where extra safety measures like masks are used. The floor should be marked with tape or paint to help people maintain social distancing. No food and drink can be consumed as part of the service, such as during a communion. Hands must be washed before and after rings are exchanged; as few people as possible to handle the rings. Couples and officiants are not allowed to speak with raised voices, such as when exchanging vows.

Raised voices should be avoided, so recordings are recommended instead of singing, and music played at a level where guests do not need to shout over it. Playing wind or blown instruments should be avoided

Mitigate risk factors by avoiding face-to-face seating, reducing the number of guests in an enclosed space, improving ventilation, using protective screen and face coverings, and restricting access to non-essential areas

Regarding receptions, the rules state: "Any receptions that typically follow or accompany marriages or civil partnerships are strongly advised not to take place at this time. "Small celebrations should only take place if following social distancing guidelines – i.e. in groups of up to two households indoors, or up to six people from different households outdoors."

From 29th June, outdoor ceremonies were allowed to take place in Scotland, with a maximum of eight guests. In Northern Ireland, ministers are now allowing outdoor weddings for up to 10 people.

The Welsh government has also lifted the ban on weddings in Wales as long as they are small enough to maintain social distancing measures.

The impact of Coronavirus on our lives has been huge, and for anyone who has a wedding planned in 2020, the current situation has thrown up a lot of questions and concerns about how their wedding day will be affected. With this latest announcement raising more questions than answers, it's still a difficult time for couples and venues as they look clarity on how weddings can go ahead.

When Will Weddings Be Allowed to Take Place Again?

Places of worship and licensed venues opened for wedding ceremonies and civil partnerships of less than 30 people were allowed from 4th July 2020 in England. The government in Northern Ireland are allowing outdoor weddings for up to 10 people, while there is no set limit on Welsh guest numbers but they must remain small enough to maintain social distancing.

As of June, indoor weddings in Scotland are still banned, and couples may only may outdoor with a maximum of eight guests.

Of Course, the situation outlined by the government and the devolved assemblies relates to this moment in time and will change over time.

****

PART ONE: CONVENTIONAL MARRIAGE GENERALLY IN THE UK.

Chapter 1

Conventional Marriage Generally In The UK

The main law governing marriage in England, The Marriage Act 1949, as amended, and The Marriage Act 1983, states that marriage is the 'voluntary union for life of one man and one woman to the exclusion of all others', although this has now been modified with the introduction of the Marriage (Same Sex Couples) Act 2013 which we discuss in Chapter 10. We will also discuss Civil Partnerships and dissolution in Chapters 3-4. We begin by discussing conventional heterosexual marriage.

Much has changed in family life over the years and today, marriages break up with alarming frequency and more and more people choose to live together as opposed to marrying.

This section is about the institution of conventional marriage and how it works within the law. We will look at who can get married, the engagement, marriage formalities, effects of marriage, cohabitation and agreements.

Marriage

The law states that, in order to marry, a person must:

a) be unmarried
b) be over the age of 18

c) a person can marry over the age of 16 with parental consent

You are also legally a single person if your previous marriage has been annulled. Basically, anyone who wants to marry must be a single person in the eyes of the law. A person must be over 18. A marriage where one of the persons is under 18 is absolutely void, unless parental consent has been gained. If someone marries between the ages of 16-18 the marriage is voidable as opposed to void (see below). Parents, guardians or the courts must consent to a marriage for someone between 16-18 years old.

The Civil Partnerships Act 2004 has introduced civil unions between same sex partners (now extended to opposite sex partners from December 31st 2019). Through a Civil Partnership, people of the same sex and also opposites sexes, acquire many of the rights of a conventional married couple. See the end of the chapter for civil partnerships and dissolution.

Although the law of conventional marriage specifies that the marriage must be between partners of opposite sexes, In 2013, the Marriage (Same sex Couples) Act was introduced which now allows same sex couples the same rights to marry as the law covering conventional marriage. There are some differences between the two laws, particularly the right to get married in a church. and this is outlined further on.

No marriage can take place between close relations, i.e. blood relations, or non-blood relations where the relation is so close that a ban on intermarriage is still imposed. Adopted children are generally treated in law as blood relatives. Brothers in law and sisters in law can marry as can stepparent and stepchild if the stepchild has not been raised as a child of the family and is over 21 years old.

Marriages must be voluntary

A marriage must be voluntary and not brought about through coercion. This brings about a problem in law when arranged marriages take place, as is the custom in certain ethnic groups. In general the law does not interfere with arranged marriages.

However, the courts will get involved if it is felt that there is duress and there is a threat of injury to life or liberty or a child is threatened with expulsion from home or community.

Forced marriage

A forced marriage is where one or both people do not (or in cases of people with learning disabilities, cannot) consent to the marriage and pressure or abuse is used. It is an appalling and indefensible practice and is recognised in the UK as a form of violence against women and men, domestic/child abuse and a serious abuse of human rights.

The pressure put on people to marry against their will can be physical (including threats, actual physical violence and sexual violence) or emotional and psychological (for example, when someone is made to feel like they're bringing shame on their

13

family). Financial abuse (taking your wages or not giving you any money) can also be a factor.

Legislation on Forced Marriage

The Anti-Social Behaviour, Crime and Policing Act 2014 makes it a criminal offence to force someone to marry. This includes:

- Taking someone overseas to force them to marry (whether or not the forced marriage takes place)
- Marrying someone who lacks the mental capacity to consent to the marriage (whether they're pressured to or not)
- Breaching a Forced Marriage Protection Order is also a criminal offence
- The civil remedy of obtaining a Forced Marriage Protection Order through the family courts will continue to exist alongside the new criminal offence, so victims can choose how they wish to be assisted

Forcing someone to marry can result in a sentence of up to 7 years in prison. Disobeying a Forced Marriage Protection Order can result in a sentence of up to 5 years in prison

Forced Marriage Unit

The Forced Marriage Unit (FMU) is a joint Foreign and Commonwealth Office and Home Office unit was which set up in January 2005 to lead on the Government's forced marriage policy, outreach and casework. It operates both inside the UK, where support is provided to any individual, and overseas, where consular assistance is provided to British nationals, including dual nationals.

The FMU operates a public helpline to provide advice and support to victims of forced marriage as well as to professionals dealing with cases. The assistance provided ranges from simple safety advice, through to aiding a victim to prevent their unwanted spouse moving to the UK ('reluctant sponsor' cases), and, in extreme circumstances, to rescues of victims held against their will overseas. See useful addresses and information for further details.

Marriages which can be annulled

Void marriages

Certain marriages are regarded in law as void. This means that, in the eyes of the law the marriage has never taken place at all. Marriages are void where:

1. Your marriage is not legally valid - 'void' marriages

You can annul a marriage if it was not legally valid in the first place, eg:

- you are closely related
- one of you was under 16
- one of you was already married or in a civil partnership
- If a marriage was not legally valid, the law says that it never existed. However, you may need legal paperwork to prove this - eg if you want to get married again.

2. Your marriage is defective - 'voidable' marriages. You can annul a marriage if:

- it wasn't consummated - you haven't had sex with the person you married since the wedding (doesn't apply for same sex couples)
- you didn't properly consent to the marriage - eg you were drunk or forced into it
- the other person had a sexually transmitted disease when you got married
- the woman was pregnant by another man when you got married

Marriages annulled for these reasons are known as 'voidable' marriages.

Getting engaged to be married

An engagement is not a precondition of marriage, as it once was. This is often the case, however. A couple will, after engagement, publicly announce their intention to be married. Legal disputes can, however, arise and couples can dispute ownership of property and gifts. An engagement ring is regarded as an outright gift in the eyes of the law.

If money has been expended on larger items, such as a house, in the anticipation of marriage, and the marriage has fallen through then this will become a legal dispute with each case turning on its own merit and the circumstances of any contract, written or unwritten. Certain insurance companies can offer insurance against weddings falling through or being cancelled. Cover can also be obtained for honeymoons falling through.

If a couples wedding falls through they are legally obliged to return any wedding gifts received to their senders.

Marriage formalities-conventional marriage

For a marriage to be valid, a formal licence and a formal ceremony are necessary. Authority to licence marriages is given to a priest of the Anglican Church and to civil officials (registrars). Every couple, therefore, must obtain permission to marry from an Anglican church or from a civil official. Many couples, because of cost, choose to marry in a registry office.

Religious ceremonies

Religious ceremonies are categorized according to whether they are solemnized by:

- The Anglican Church, including the Church of Wales
- Jews or Quakers (for whom special rules apply under the Marriage Act 1949
- Some other recognized religion.

Church of England-licence to marry

About half of all religious marriage ceremonies take place in the Church of England. There are four ways to effect the necessary preliminaries for an Anglican marriage. Only one may be used. In order to obtain consent to marry in the Church of England you must either:

- publish banns

or obtain one of the following:

- a common ecclesiastical licence
- a 'special licence, also from the ecclesiastical authorities
- a superintendent registrars certificate from the civil authorities.

Publishing banns

The banns, or the names of the couple who intend to marry, have to be read aloud (published) in the church of the parish where the couple are resident. If the couple are resident in different parishes then the banns must be read in each parish church, in one or other of which the ceremony will take place. The priest needs seven days notice in writing from both parties before the banns can be read. The priest has to read them audibly in church on three successive Sundays. If there is no objection from any member of the congregation then, after the third reading the marriage can take place. If any objections are raised, and voiced audibly by a member of the congregation then the banns are void.

Common licence

This dispenses with the banns and is given by the Bishop of the diocese. You must make a sworn affidavit that there is no impediment to the marriage and that any necessary parental consent has been given and that you have resided in the parish for 15 days.

Once granted, the licence to marry has immediate effect and is valid for three months. It will specify the church or chapel in which the marriage is to take place.

Special licence

This is issued by the Archbishop of Canterbury and enables a marriage to take place at any time or place. It also dispenses with the 15-day residence period. To get such a licence, which would for example be applicable if one of the parties was seriously ill, a sworn statement is required.

Superintendent registrars certificate

Although it is the norm for a marriage in the Church of England to take place after banns have been read, or after obtaining a licence from church authorities, an Anglican wedding can take place after a superintendent registrars certificate has been obtained. The parties must give notice to a superintendent registrar in the district in which they have resided for at least seven days before giving notice. They must make a solemn declaration that there are no lawful impediments to their union and that they meet the residential requirements. In the case of persons between 16-18, that they have parental consent. If the parties live in different districts then notice must be given in each district.

The notice is displayed in the superintendent's office for 21 days. At the end of that period, provided there are no objections, the certificate is issued. The marriage can take place in a church within the superintendent's district. The consent of the minister of the church must be obtained.

Divorced person wishing to marry in the Church of England

Where either party is a divorced person, a remarriage cannot be solemnized in the Church of England. However, since 2002, a vicar of a church can make the decision to allow a remarriage in church. This does not apply where the marriage has been annulled.

Other stipulations to a Church of England wedding are laid down in the law, as follows:

- the marriage must be in an unlocked church
- between the hours of 8am and 8pm
- two witnesses must be present

Other denominations and religions

If you belong to another denomination or religion other than the Church of England, you must first obtain permission from the civil authorities to marry. There are four ways of meeting the legal requirements, of which only one need be used:

- a superintendent registrars certificate

- a superintendent registrars certificate with a licence. This has a residence requirement of 15 days.

For those seriously ill or detained, special provisions under the Marriage Act 1983 and the Marriage (Registrar General's Licence) Act 1970 will apply.

Weddings for Jews and Quakers can take place anywhere or at any time under the Marriage Act according to their own practices. The marriage is solemnized by a person designated for the purpose.

Civil ceremonies

The General Register Office will issue a form which provides notes on the legal formalities of marrying. Marriages in a register office require a solemn declaration from both bride and groom according to the civil form:

- that they know of no impediment to their union
- that they can call upon those present as witnesses that they take each other as lawful wedded wife or husband.

The two witnesses present then sign the register.

The superintendent registrar and the registrar must both be present at a civil wedding, which can only take place in a registry office, except in very unusual circumstances where people are ill or otherwise confined.

Witnesses

All marriages, without exception, be they religious or civil, require two witnesses to the ceremony. The witnesses need not know the couple. After a ceremony the witnesses sign the register and a marriage certificate is issued.

Marriages abroad

Generally speaking, a marriage that takes place in another country is recognised as valid in this country. However, all the laws associated with marriage in England and Wales, must apply, such as the age restriction and the single person status. It is essential if a person intends to marry abroad that they seek legal advice in order to ascertain the status of the marriage in the UK.

Effects of a marriage

Being married confers a legal status on husband and wife. In general, questions of status, rights and duties concern the following:

Duty to live together

Husband and wife have a duty to live together. If one spouse leaves the other for good then an irretrievable breakdown has occurred (see next chapter on divorce).

Duty to maintain

Spouses have a duty to maintain one another. This extends to children, obviously, and becomes a particular problem on breakdown of marriage.

Sexual relationship

Husband and wife are expected to have sexual relations. Failure to consummate a marriage, as we have seen, can lead to annulment of a marriage.

Fidelity

Husband and wife are expected to be faithful to one another. Adultery is one of the main grounds for divorce.

Surnames

A wife can take her husbands surname but is not under a legal duty to do so. A wife's right to use the husbands surname will survive death and divorce. A husband can also take a wife's surname although this is unusual.

Occasionally, couples will adopt both surnames. If a wife changes her surname to her husbands she can do so informally, simply by using the name. However, change of surname has to be declared to institutions such as banks and a marriage certificate has to be produced.

Joint assets

The matrimonial home as well as family income become assets of a marriage. As we will see, a breakdown of marriage can lead to long and costly battles over assets of a marriage.

*

Common parenthood

Husband and wife automatically acquire parental responsibility for the children of their marriage. If the couple separate the courts can alter the relationship between parent and child.

Marital confidences

Secrets and other confidences of married life shared between husband and wife are protected by law. This is particularly relevant in this day and age where the tabloids invade the lives of people as never before. Married, and even divorced, persons can obtain injunctions to stop publication of confidential information.

Marriages of convenience

The laws surrounding such marriages have been gradually tightening up. Such marriages are seen as sham devices to get around UK immigration law. In order to issue a person with an entry clearance certificate to enter the UK as an affianced person or spouse, the immigration authorities will want to be sure that:

a) the 'primary' purpose is to get married and that a separation will not take place after marriage and entry

b) that spouses intend to live together as husband and wife

c) if the couple are not already married that the marriage will take place within six months.

It also has to be shown that parties to the marriage will settle in the UK.

Cohabitation

Despite peoples perceptions to the contrary, there is no such thing as 'common law' relationships, i.e. people living together unmarried, as man and wife. As far as the law is concerned they are two legal individuals. There is no duty to cohabit, no duty to maintain. With regard to children, the duty of care usually falls on the mother. However, in the case of unmarried couples, both mother and father can enter into a parental responsibility agreement which should place them in a similar position to married couples in regards to responsibility for children.

If a couple who cohabit and have children, do separate then there is a duty on the father (absent parent) to maintain the child until they reach the age of 17.

Effect on assets

The courts can decide what split will take place in regard to assets of a cohabiting couple. This share is based on concrete facts of the individual's contributions. A live-in partner has no right to occupy the family home under the Matrimonial Homes Act 1973, in the event of breakdown of relationship. However, the law has tightened up in this area.

*

Taxation

There are important differences between the tax position of married and cohabiting couples. These are as follows:

- cohabiting couples cannot take advantage of the taxation rules between husband and wife that ensure gifts between husband and wife are free of capital gains tax
- they cannot take advantage of the fact that on the death of a spouse, the other spouse inherits free of inheritance tax

However, as these rules change frequently you should refer to your local tax office for advice. You should also take advice concerning wills and pensions.

Where the law treats cohabitees as husband and wife

There are certain areas where the law will afford the same protection to cohabitees as married people:

- Victims of domestic violence are entitled to protection whether married or not
- With regard to security of tenure, a couple who live together as husband and wife will be entitled to joint security whether married or not
- Certain social security benefits are available for live-in couples. You should seek advice from the local benefits agency
- A duty to maintain the children of a relationship is imposed-irrespective of whether married or not

- Under the Fatal Accidents Act 1976 dependant cohabitees, who have lived together for two years or more may be entitled to damages on his or her death.

Agreements

Cohabitees can enter into agreements to protect property and other assets in the event of splitting up. Married couples also do this.

Contracts between married couples

At common law, a husband 'administered' his wife's property. In effect, a woman no longer owned property after she married. The law moves on thankfully! Today, property that a woman owned before marriage remains her own. If divorce takes place the question to be considered is whether the property has become an asset of the marriage. Each case will turn on its own merit.

In view of the courts wide powers to determine what happens to assets after marriage, few couples enter into agreements (pre-nuptial agreement being the most common). However, the wealthier the person, the wiser it is to enter into such an agreement.

Prenuptial agreements

Prenuptial agreements were not traditionally regarded as binding by the English divorce courts, but there are signs of change. One factor behind this is the increasingly international character of people's lives. So saying this, the main aim behind prenuptial agreements is that, for at least one of the parties to marriage, be it man or woman, may wish to preserve previously acquired assets from the jurisdiction of the divorce courts. Unfortunately, the situation in almost all cases is that the jurisdiction of the courts cannot be ousted in this way and prenuptial agreements are quite often not worth the paper they are written on.

The agreement will be considered in the light of exactly how long the marriage has lasted and also whether or not there are children involved. English courts traditionally would say that the husband or wife should part with some of the pre-existing wealth if the assets built up over a marriage did not suffice to provide for children's well being.

One relatively recent case which serves to highlight the changes referred to is that of Radmacher v Grantino. Mr Grantino, a French national, married Ms Radmacher, a German national in 1998. The marriage lasted until 2006. They had two children by their marriage. Ms Radmacher belonged to a wealthy industrial family. They came to live in England and sought a divorce in England. By the time of the divorce it was estimated that Ms Radmacher was worth £100m. Much of the wife's wealth had been given to her by her family during her marriage. Prior to the marriage, the wife's family were concerned that none of the wealth should go to her husband so an agreement was drawn up, in a German court. This was drawn up in German, and in the context of German law and Mr Grantino had no real input into the agreement. At the time of the divorce Mr Grantino was claiming £5m for himself and children to ensure that the children were cared for. The court of appeal stated that adults ought to be free to make their own arrangements. They decided that although Ms Radmacher should buy her husband a house he would only have the right to occupy it while the children were dependant.

The case then moved onto the Supreme Court who upheld the view of the Appeal Court and that Mr Grantino should be held to the terms of the prenuptial agreement. However, this case involved millions of pounds whereas most don't and the courts will continue to look at prenuptial agreements on their own merits.

Changes to the law

Following Law Commission proposals, first published in 2014, with a draft Bill, it was expected that pre-nups will become enshrined in law. Policy-makers will probably include safe-guards so that neither spouse is left in need in the event of divorce, and will recommend that both parties take independent legal advice. a person won't be able to keep their business intact using a pre-nup if it means leaving a wife of 20 years without proper provision, for example.

Cohabitation agreement

When unmarried couples part, the courts have little powers to determine the split of assets. In relation to cohabitation agreements, there are problems under the law of contract. When parties enter into a contract, both sides have to offer something towards the contract. This is called 'consideration' for the contract. In an agreement to cohabit it would be difficult to define consideration other than on the basis of a sexual relationship. Nevertheless it is wise to have an agreement as a basis, or structure, of the relationship when it concerns assets.

The Marriage (Same Sex Couples) Act 2013
The Marriage (Same Sex Couples) Act 2013 came into force on 17 July 2013 and allows same-sex couples the same right to marry as opposite-sex couples. This is discussed in more detail in chapter 10.

Briefly, Ceremonies can take place in any civil venue and religious organisations will have the opportunity to "opt in" to performing religious same-sex marriages. However, the Church of England and the Church in Wales are specifically prevented by the legislation from conducting same-sex marriages.

The 2013 Act remains separate from the Marriage Act 1949, which allows opposite-sex couples to marry, although the provisions are largely the same and afford married same-sex couples the same legal status as married opposite-sex couples. The term "marriage" and "married couple" is now extended to include same-sex couples.

****

Chapter 2

Divorce or Dissolution-Main Principles of the Law

Divorce law generally

I will deal with the (slight differences) between heterosexual couples and same-sex couples when it comes to ending a marriage or civil partnership at the end of the chapter. These will be elaborated upon in the respective chapters. Most of the law, and the subsequent financial and child related issues affecting divorce, dissolution of Civil Partnerships or Same-Sex Marriages is similar and applies to both.

Divorce law has developed over the years through legislation made by Parliament and through the build up of "precedents" or through cases decided by the courts. However, in the last thirty years there have been fundamental changes in the way society, and the law, has come to view divorce.

Modern divorce law recognizes that "irretrievable breakdown" of a marriage should be the one and only ground for divorce. This recognition signalled a move away from the idea of "guilty parties" in divorce.

The Divorce, Dissolution and Separation Act 2020

The Divorce, Dissolution and Separation Bill became an Act of Parliament on 25 June 2020. It is however expected to take some time to implement; the Lord Chancellor, Robert Buckland, has suggested that it should come into force in the autumn of 2021.

Once in force, couples will be able to obtain a divorce without one party being required to attribute blame to the other.

Either or both parties, will be able to apply to the Court for a 'Divorce Order'; the application must be accompanied by a statement confirming that the marriage has irretrievably broken down.

The applicant(s) will be required to confirm to the Courts after 20 weeks, that they wish for their application to continue, so that a Conditional Order can be made; and 6 weeks thereafter the Courts can grant a Divorce Order, dissolving the marriage.

The 26-week period between application and divorce has sparked some debate, but overall the Bill is a very welcome update for family lawyers. After 30 years of campaigning by Resolution and other groups, the Bill is a step towards minimising the negative impact of divorce on parties, their children, and family lives more generally.

*

Before the introduction of the notion of irretrievable breakdown it was held that one party had to prove that the other party was guilty of destroying the marriage before divorce could be granted. The law is now much more flexible in its recognition of the breakdown of a marriage.

Since the present law was introduced, making it much easier to obtain divorce, the number of marriage breakdowns in Britain has risen significantly, with one in three couples filing for divorce. This is currently the highest rate in Europe.

There are a lot of problems associated with the law, and the role of those who make divorce law generally. The whole question of divorce law is under scrutiny, particularly the question of whether or not the law should attempt to keep marriages intact or whether it should seek to ease the transition to final separation without presenting unnecessary obstacles. However, although we hear periodic announcements from different politicians on the importance of keeping the family unit intact, and by implication making it harder for people to divorce, the whole climate has changed over the years whereby the law seems to be the facilitator of divorce as opposed to dictating whether or not people can get a divorce.

There has also been a major shift in the law concerning children of divorcing couples. Under The Children Act 1989 (as amended), parents in divorce proceedings are encouraged to take the initiative and take matters into their own hands, making their own decisions concerning the child's future life after divorce. The courts role has been greatly restricted.

The Child Support Act 1991 (as amended by the 1995 CSA) has also dramatically changed the role of the courts in divorce proceedings. The Child Maintenance Service, assesses and determines applications for maintenance in accordance with a set formula. The courts will only now deal with applications for maintenance in certain circumstances.

Law generally – the courts

Before looking at the law surrounding divorce in greater depth, we should look briefly at the structure of the courts and how divorce law is administered.

County courts

Most divorces are handled by a branch of the county court system known as the divorce county courts.

County courts are local courts, usually found within towns and cities throughout England and Wales. These courts do not deal with criminal matters but they attempt to find solutions to virtually every other type of problem facing people in every day life. Such problems might be those that arise between businesses and their customers, between neighbours and between landlord and tenant, to name but a few. Decisions concerning divorce cases, and subsequent orders, were made by Judges and District Judges. However, since 2017, and a reorganisation of the Divorce Courts, a centralisation has meant that 47 Regional Courts were reduced to just 11 divorce centres. Most uncontested decree nisi applications are now considered by legal advisors rather than district judges. This has led, inevitably, in a slowdown and one criticism is that divorces, particularly 'quickie' divorces are taking longer to finalise. In particular, with the COVID 19 pandemic the process is very much slower.

In addition to the judges and legal advisors there is also a large staff of officials who provide the administrative machinery of the courts. Like all administrators, they are the backbone of the operation.

The High Court

Sometimes, rarely, divorce cases need to be referred to the High Court. There are several sections of the high court-the section responsible for divorce and other similar matters is known as the Family Division. However, the majority of divorce cases will be heard in the county courts.

Hearing your divorce case

Hearings related to divorce cases are either in "Open" court or in "Chambers". Proceedings in open court are heard in the court-room itself. They are usually formal and members of the public are allowed to attend. However, most divorces are heard in chambers. These proceedings are private and the general public has no right to attend or listen. Only those people directly concerned with the case are allowed to attend.

Same sex couples-grounds for divorce

For the most part, the grounds for divorce in same sex marriages are the same, but, as stated, a same sex marriage cannot rely on adultery because the definition of adultery is 'engaging in sexual intercourse with a person of the opposite sex.

Therefore if a gay couple separated because one of them went off with a member of the same sex, they could not rely on adultery – it would have to be 'unreasonable behaviour'."

Generally

The first question facing couples that wish to divorce is whether or not they qualify at the outset to bring proceedings, i.e., what are the ground rules. If one or other parties wishes to file for divorce, the most basic requirement that must be fulfilled is that they should have been married for one-year minimum. They must also be "domiciled" in this country. Both parties must have their permanent homes in England or Wales when the petition is started or both parties should be living in either England or Wales when the petition is started. If this is not the case then both parties must have had their last home in England or Wales when the petition is started or must have been living in England or Wales for at least a year on the day the petition is started. There are a few other stipulations concerning domicile. Leaflet D183 which can be found on the www.justice.gov.uk website explains domicile in depth.

A court can halt proceedings for divorce in England if it would be better for the case to be heard in another country. Usually, the court would try to decide which country is the most appropriate, or with which country the divorcing couple are most closely associated.

Grounds for divorce – the 'five facts'.

As we have seen (although soon to change), currently there is only one ground for granting a divorce, that is the irretrievable breakdown of marriage. Fundamentally, this means that your marriage has broken down to such a degree that it cannot be retrieved and the only solution is to end it legally. (Matrimonial Causes Act 1973).

The person, or spouse, who requests a divorce is known as the "petitioner". the other party is known as the "respondent".

Although there is only one ground for divorce, the court has to be satisfied that there is clear evidence of one of the following five facts:

1. that the respondent has committed adultery and the petitioner cannot, or finds it intolerable, to live with the respondent;

2. that the respondent has behaved in such a way that you cannot reasonably be expected to live with him or her (unreasonable behaviour)

3. that the respondent has deserted you for a continuous period of two years immediately before the presentation of your petition for divorce.

4. that parties to a marriage have lived apart for more than two years prior to filing for divorce and that there is no objection or defence to filing for divorce. This is known as the "no fault" ground;

5. that parties to marriage have lived apart continuously five years prior to filing for divorce.

We should now look at each of these "five facts" in more depth.

1. Adultery

Quite simply, adultery is defined as heterosexual sex between one party to a marriage and someone else.

Adultery usually means that a "full" sexual act has been committed so therefore if there has not been penetration then this will not be seen to be adulterous.

For adultery to be proved, an admission by the respondent or evidence of adultery is usually sufficient. The co-respondent need not be named in the divorce petition. If you do mention the name of the co-respondent involved in the adultery, that person is entitled to take part in the divorce proceedings in so far as they affect them. The court will provide the co-respondent with copies of all the relevant divorce papers and he or she will have the opportunity to confirm or deny anything said about him or her in the divorce proceedings.

Proving adultery is the first step. You then have to satisfy the courts that you find it intolerable to live with the respondent any further. However, it is not essential to prove that you find it intolerable to live with the respondent because of their adultery. It may be that your marriage has been unhappy for some time and that the adulterous act has proven to be the end. If, after you discover the respondent's adultery, you continue to live together as man and wife for a period of six months or more, you will not be able to rely on adultery as a reason for divorce. As long as the periods of living together after the adultery do not exceed six months in total, the courts will completely disregard them. This gives some room for attempts at reconciliation.

2. Unreasonable behaviour

Although "unreasonable behaviour" is a commonly cited fact for divorce, in practice the court has stringent criteria, which must be met before this is accepted. The law actually says that you must demonstrate that your spouse has behaved in such a way that you cannot reasonably be expected to continue to live with that person. The court considering your case will look at the particular circumstances surrounding your situation and will then decide whether or not you should continue to tolerate your partner's behaviour within marriage.

The main principle underlying unreasonable behaviour is that it is particular to your own situation and that it cannot be seen as relative to other people's behaviour.

You must prove that the behaviour of your partner has gone well beyond the kind of day-to-day irritations that many people suffer and there is real reason to grant a divorce.

Examples of such behaviour range from continuous violence and threatening or intimidating behaviour, drunkenness, sexual perversions, neglect, and imposing unreasonable restrictions on another person.

3. Desertion

The fact that you must prove that your spouse has deserted you for a continuous period of two years can present difficulties.

If you are seeking a divorce on the basis of desertion, then it is likely that you will need to employ a solicitor who will need to check rigorously that you comply with the (often complex) requirements upon which a court will insist before granting a divorce. In the main, desertion has arisen because of other associated problems within marriage, and therefore this factor can often be joined with others when applying for a divorce

The simplest form of desertion is when one person walks out on another for no apparent reason. Desertion, however, is not just a physical separation of husband and wife. It implies that the deserting party has rejected all the normal obligations associated with marriage.

Before desertion is proven a court will need to be satisfied of two things:

1. You must demonstrate that you and your spouse have been living separately for a continuous period of two years immediately before you started the divorce proceedings. Although it is usual for separation to start when one person leaves the marital home, it can also happen whilst you are living under the same roof, but living totally separate lives.

The courts are very rigorous indeed when determining that this is the case and will need to be satisfied that your lives are indeed separate and that you can no longer go on carrying out functions jointly. The court will disregard short periods during the separation where you may have attempted to patch up your differences. However, for example, if you attempt to reconcile six months into the initial two year period and this lasts for two months before you separate again, although the courts will not make you start again they will make you wait a further two months before they will hear your divorce. Therefore, the two years becomes two years and two months.

2. That your spouse has decided that your marriage is over-you must also be able to demonstrate that when he or she stopped living with you, your spouse viewed the marriage as ended and intended to separate from you on a permanent basis.

You will not be able to claim desertion if you consented to the separation. The court will take consent to mean that you made it clear from the outset that you consented to separation, through your words or actions.

In addition, you will not be able to claim desertion if your spouse had perfectly good reason to leave, for example he or she may have gone abroad with your full knowledge, to work or may have entered hospital for a long period.

If your spouse leaves because of your own unreasonable behaviour, then you cannot claim desertion. If you are to blame in this case, the courts will not accept desertion.

Finally, because the courts see desertion as essentially separation against your will, then if you come back together again on a permanent basis you can no longer claim desertion.

4. Separation for two years with consent

As with desertion, the particular circumstances in which the law looks upon you as having been separated for two years can include periods of time where you may have been under the same roof together but not functioning as a married couple. There may be short periods during this time where you have lived together, for example, an attempt at reconciliation.

However, as with desertion you will not be able to count these periods towards the two years separation. Therefore, if you have a trial reconciliation period for three months then you will have to wait two years and three months before you can apply for divorce.

The fundamental difference between desertion and separation with consent is that you would not be granted a divorce on the basis of separation if your spouse did not give his or her consent to the divorce.

The court has rigid criteria for proving that your spouse consents to the divorce. Consent is only seen as valid if your spouse has freely given it without pressure. There must also be full understanding on his or her part of what a divorce will mean and how it will affect his or her life.

The court sends a form to divorcing parties soon after initial divorce papers are filed, together with explanatory notes and it is at this point when your spouse will give consent. If your spouse will not consent to divorce and you cannot prove either desertion or adultery then you will be in the position where you will have to wait until five years separation has elapsed before you can seek a divorce. In relation to the above, i.e., divorces granted on the basis of two years separation and consent or five years separation, the courts can exercise special powers to ensure that the financial and personal position of the respondent is protected. The courts can sometimes delay the process of divorce, or even prevent it, to make sure that there is no undue suffering or exploitation.

5. Five years separation

The final of the "five facts" is the fact of five years separation. If you have been separated for five or more years the courts will grant a divorce whether or not the other party agrees to it, subject to what has been said above. Again, the courts will allow for a period of attempted reconciliation up to six months and the same rules concerning length of time apply as with the other facts. Should you live together for longer than six months, the courts will demand that you start the five-year period again.

Reconciliation

As been shown, in all the provisions of the law relating to each of the five facts which have to be demonstrated in addition to the main ground of "irretrievable breakdown", there are built in provisions for reconciliation. The law is fairly flexible when taking into account attempts at reconciling and sorting out differences.

In effect, these built in provisions allow for a period of up to six months in which both parties can make a concerted attempt at solving their problems. If these attempts are unsuccessful then their legal position vis-a-vis divorce proceedings will not be jeopardized. The reconciliation provisions apply for a period up to six months or separate periods not exceeding six months.

In addition to this, a solicitor, if you have one, will need to certify that he or she has discussed the possibility of reconciliation with you and has ensured that both parties know where to seek advice and guidance if they really wish to attempt reconciliation. The court, if it so wishes, can also adjourn proceedings to give both parties further time to decide whether they genuinely wish to make a further effort to prolong their marriage.

At the end of this book can be found names and addresses of various organizations which can help with the process of reconciliation. The best known of these is RELATE.

Alternative Dispute Resolution-conciliation and mediation services

There is a fundamental difference between reconciliation, and those services which offer help, and Alternative Dispute Resolution.

Conciliation is directed towards making parting easier to handle. The role of the conciliator is to sort out at least some of the difficulties between those who have made a definite and firm decision to obtain a divorce.

The process of conciliation can take place either out of court, or in court. In court, conciliation only arises once the process of litigating for divorce has commenced. It is particularly relevant where the future of children is under discussion.

With in-court conciliation, there is usually what is known as a "pre trial review" of the issues and problems which parties to a divorce are unable to settle themselves. Both the court welfare officer and the district judge are involved in this process.

Out of court conciliation and mediation is intended to assist both parties in reaching an agreement at a stage before they arrive in court, or approach the court. The person involved at this stage is usually always professionally trained, a social worker normally, and who will act as go between. Both parties can also use specially trained legal personnel, lawyers, to help them reach an agreement. This process is like the process of arbitration and is intended to make the formal legal proceedings less hostile and acrimonious. The Ministry of Justice provides details about mediation services local to you.

Couples heading to the divorce courts will have to consider mediation before legally separating. As part of reforms included in the Children and Families Act 2014, anyone seeking a court order to resolve a dispute over children, finances or splitting property must attend a "mediation information and assessment meeting".

The Family Mediation Council will help and assist in this area https://www.familymediationcouncil.org.uk. The Family Mediation Council was established in October 2007 and works for greater public awareness of, and access to, family mediation. They work closely with the Legal Aid Agency (LAA) and the Ministry of Justice (MoJ) on family mediation related projects.

*

Dissolution of a Civil Partnership

A petition can be filed 12 months after the initial registration of a civil partnership but one of four conditions must be proved:

- The other person has behaved unreasonably;
- The parties have been separated for two years and the other party consents in writing;
- The other party has deserted you for a period of two years;
- You have been separated for five years, consent is then not necessary.

To end a civil partnership, you first need to fill in a dissolution application.

You must include your:

- full name and address
- civil partner's full name and address
- civil partnership certificate - send the original certificate or get a copy from a register office
- Include the names and dates of birth of any children (no matter how old they are).
- You must try to find your civil partner's current address if you do not know it. The court will need it to send them a copy of the dissolution application.

Because of coronavirus (COVID-19), applications to end a civil partnership are taking longer than usual to process.

Pay the court fee

You will have to pay a £550 court fee to file the dissolution application.

Financial Claims

The court has the power to make a financial order for payment of a lump sum, transfer of property, pension sharing order and maintenance.

On the death of a civil partner the rights of succession are the same as those given to the survivor of a marriage.

Marriage (Same Sex Couples) Act 2013

This act makes provision for same sex couples in England and Wales. It makes marriage between same sex couples lawful and equivalent to a marriage between a man and woman. The term husband will include a man married to another man. The term wife will include a woman married to another woman.

Persons of the same sex will not be able to divorce on adultery or have their marriage annulled for non-consummation.

The grounds for divorce between a same sex couple are the same as those between a man and a woman save a divorce cannot be filed on the basis of adultery. There is one ground – that the marriage has broken down irretrievably and then one or more of four facts needs to be proved:

• Unreasonable behaviour of the other person;

- Desertion by the other person for a period of two years or more;
- Two years separation with the other party's consent in writing;
- Five years separation where no consent is needed.

In a same sex marriage, the parties have the same rights to make an application for financial provision. The court has power to make an order for maintenance, lump sum, transfer of property and pension provision.

****

PART TWO: CIVIL PARTNERSHIPS IN THE UK

Chapter 3.

An Overview of the Civil Partnership Act 2004 as Amended by the Civil Partnership Regulations (Opposite Sex Couples) 2019

The following introduction provides an overview of the Civil Partnerships Act 2004 as amended. It is intended to provide a background to the more detailed information provided within the body of the text contained in this book.

The book does not cover Scotland or Northern Ireland, which are contained in Parts 3 and 4 to the Act, although there are references to both countries throughout. The Act is similar throughout the United Kingdom, but there are differences which take into account different legal systems. For further details on the Act as it applies in Scotland and Northern Ireland you should go to the government website which displays the Act in its entirety: www. legislation.gov.uk.

Since 2005, the number of civil partnerships has naturally declined, and the differences in men and women entering civil partnerships has equalised. With the introduction of the Marriage (Same Sex Couples) Act 2013 as described in Chapter 11, the trend has been that more couples opt to get married, although it remains to be seen whether this trend will continue.

The Civil Partnership Regulations (Opposite Sex Couples) 2019 and the Civil Partnerships, Marriages and Deaths (Registration etc) Act 2019

As of 31st December 2019, it is now possible for both same-sex and heterosexual couples to enter into a civil partnership. The Civil Partnerships, Marriages and Deaths (Registration etc) Act 2019 makes provision about the registration of marriage; to make provision for the extension of civil partnerships to couples not of the same sex; to make provision for a report on the registration of pregnancy loss; to make provision about the investigation of still-births; and for connected purposes.

The institution was initially devised solely for same-sex couples through the Civil Partnership Act 2004; it was meant to be a distinct separate relationship status for same-sex couples akin, but different to, a marriage. This has now changed and moving into 2020, heterosexual couples may opt for a civil partnership instead of a marriage.

There are a number of important points to note in view of this change in law. It is right to say that a civil partnership offers a genuine alternative for heterosexual couples to marriage; certainly in the key case of Steinfeld & Keidan, the landmark case in this area, the applicants emphasised the importance of couples having a secular alternative to marriage.

From a legal perspective, couples who opt to enter into a civil partnership should consider a pre-partnership agreement. These agreements, usually known as 'pre-nups', set out the terms of financial settlement on divorce, and can now can be drafted to apply in the context of dissolution of a heterosexual civil partnership. Of course, they still remain available to same-sex couples.

The drafting of this type of arrangement of course should be done to protect assets and provide clarity on what is to happen if parties separate. They are not legally binding, but they are heavily persuasive and help to route to mitigate the risk of contentious litigation on separation. On this point, heterosexual couples who do enter into civil partnerships should note that they are then, on separation, subject to the same principles as divorcing couples if an application to court is required to deal with financial issues. We expect a large number of pre-partnership agreements in the next few years and thereafter, given this recent change in the law as well as more awareness around the topic.

*

Civil Partnerships generally-the 2004 Act

Part 1 of the Civil Partnerships Act 2004 (as amended by the Civil Partnership Regulations (Same Sex Couples) 2019 introduces and defines a civil partnership.

A Civil partnership is a legal relationship, which can be registered by two people of the same sex. Same sex couples within a civil partnership can obtain legal recognition for their relationship and can obtain the same benefits generally as married couples.

The Civil Partnerships Act came into force on 5th December 2005. The first civil partnerships registered in England and Wales took place on 21st December 2005. Civil partners will be treated the same as married couples in many areas, including:

- Tax, including inheritance tax
- Employment benefits
- Most state and occupational pension benefits
- Income related benefits, tax credits and child support
- Maintenance for partner and children
- Ability to apply for parental responsibility for a child
- Inheritance of a tenancy agreement
- Recognition under intestacy rules
- Access to fatal accidents compensation
- Protection from domestic violence
- Recognition for immigration and nationality purposes

The registration of a civil partnership

Part 2, Chapter 1, of the Act introduces the registration process. Two people may register a civil partnership provided they are of the same sex, not already in a civil partnership or legally married, not closely related and both over 16 although consent of a parent or guardian must be obtained if either of them are under 18. This section of the Act has now been amended by Paragraph 34 of the Marriage (Same Sex Persons) Act 2013 which now states that a widow or widower under 18 does not require consent of another person before entering into a civil partnership.

54

Registering a civil partnership is a secular procedure and is carried out by the registration service, which is responsible for the registration of births, deaths and marriages. A civil partnership registration is carried out under what is termed a standard procedure, which can be varied to take into account housebound people or people who are ill and are not expected to recover.

The standard procedure for registering a civil partnership

A couple wishing to register a civil partnership just have to decide the date they want to register and where they want the registration to take place. The formal process for registering consists of two main stages-the giving of a notice of intention to register and then the registration of the civil partnership itself.

The first stage, the giving of notice is a legal requirement and both partners have to do this at a register office in the area of a local authority where they live, even if they intend to register elsewhere. The notice contains the names, age, marital or civil partnership status, address, occupation, nationality and intended venue for the civil partnership. It is a criminal offence to give false information. If one of the partners is a non-EEA citizen and subject to immigration controls (see later) there are additional requirements to be fulfilled. Once the notice has been given it is displayed at the relevant register office for 28 days. This provides an opportunity for objections to be made. The civil partnership cannot be registered until after 28 clear days have elapsed from the date of the second person gives notice.

Each partner needs to give notice in the area that they have lived for at least seven days. If the couple live in different areas then each will post a notice in their own relevant area. When giving notice they will be asked where they wish the civil partnership to take place.

Residency requirements for a civil partnerships

A couple can register a civil partnership in England and Wales as long as they have both lived in a registration district in England and Wales for at least seven days immediately before giving notice. If one person lives in Scotland and the other lives in England or Wales, the person living in Scotland may give notice there. Officers, sailors or marines on board a Royal Navy ship at sea can give notice to the captain or other commanding officer, providing they are going to register with someone who is resident in England and Wales. Service personnel based outside England and Wales have to fulfil the above residence requirements.

Documentary evidence of name, age and nationality will need to be shown. Passports and birth certificates are the main documents required. Proof of address will be required. If either partner has been married or in a civil partnership before, then evidence of divorce or dissolution will be required. If either partner is subject to immigration control a document showing entry clearance granted to form a civil partnership will need to be shown, along with a home office certificate of approval and indefinite leave to remain in the UK.

Civil partnership registration

A civil partnership registration can take place in any register office in England and Wales or at any venue that has been approved to hold a civil partnership. Approved premises include stately homes and other prestigious buildings including hotels and restaurants. From 5th December 2005, any venue that has approval for civil marriage will automatically be approved for civil partnerships. A civil partnership cannot be registered on a religious premises unless the premises has been approved by a local authority and permission has been given by the local authority. A civil partnership can only be registered between the hours of 8am to 6pm unless one person is seriously ill and is not expected to recover.

A civil partnership is legally registered once the couple have signed the legal document, known as a civil partnership schedule, in the presence of a registrar and two witnesses. On the day, two witnesses will be required. If they wish to do so, the couple will be able to speak to each other the words contained in the schedule:

' I declare that I know of no legal reason why we may not register as each other's civil partner. I understand that on signing this document we will be forming a civil partnership with each other'

A ceremony can be arranged to accompany the actual registration. This ceremony can take place at any venue as long

57

as it is approved. It is prohibited for civil partnerships to include religious readings, music or symbols.

As stated above, it was originally prohibited for the ceremonies to take place in religious venues. On 17 February 2011, Her Majesty's Government announced that, as the result of the passing of the Equality Act 2010, it would bring forward the necessary measures to remove the latter restriction in England and Wales, although religious venues would not be compelled to offer civil partnerships. This was implemented by The Marriages and Civil Partnerships (Approved Premises) (Amendment) Regulations 2011

Costs of registering a civil partnership
The costs here are applicable to 2020/21. Like all other costs they will change from year to year and the current costs should always be ascertained by contacting your local register office. The current average costs are as follows:

- Giving notice of intention to register   £35 (£70 per couple)
- Registration at Register Office   £50

Registration at an approved premises-in this case the cost for attendance by a civil partnership registrar is set by the registration authority in question. A further charge may also be made by the owner for use of the building,

- Cost of civil partnership certificate on the day of registration (Average) £4
- Further copies of the civil partnership certificate (Average) £10

The General Register Office website www.gro.gov.uk has a search facility if you need to find a local register office or an office any where in the UK.

Changing names

After registering a civil partnership, one partner might want to change their surname to that of their partner. Government departments and agencies will accept civil partnership certificates as evidence for changing surnames. Other private institutions may want a different form of evidence. It is up to the individual to check with the various organisations if they wish to change their surname.

Special circumstances

Variations to the standard procedure can be made in certain circumstances. If a partner is seriously ill and is not expected to recover then a civil partnership can be registered at any time. The 28-day waiting period will not apply. A certificate will need to be provided from a doctor stating that a person is not expected to recover and cannot be moved to a place where civil partnerships take place and that they understand the nature and purpose of signing the Registrar Generals licence.

Housebound people

If one partner is housebound there are special procedures to allow them to register a civil partnership at home. A statement has to be signed, made by a doctor, confirming that this is the case and that the condition is likely to continue for the next three months. The statement must have been made no more than 14 days before notice being given and must be made on a standard form provided by the register office. The normal 28-day period will apply between giving notice and the civil partnership registration.

Detained people

There are special procedures to allow a couple to register a civil partnership at a place where one of them is detained in a hospital or prison. The couple have to provide a statement, made by the prison governor or responsible person confirming that the place where a person is detained can be named in the notice of proposed civil partnership as the place where the registration is to take place. This statement must have been made no more than 21 days prior to notice being given. The normal 28 day waiting period applies.

Gender change

The Gender Recognition Act 2004 enables transsexual people to change their legal gender by obtaining a full Gender Recognition Certificate. You can stay married if you apply for a Gender

Recognition Certificate, unless your marriage is registered under the law of Northern Ireland.

You and your spouse must fill in a statutory declaration saying you both agree to stay married.

You'll get an 'interim certificate' if you or your spouse don't want to remain married, or if neither of you fill in a statutory declaration. You can use the interim certificate as grounds to end the marriage.

If you live in England or Wales, you'll only get a full certificate once you end your marriage.

If your marriage was registered in Scotland, you can use an interim certificate to apply to the sheriff court for a full certificate. You don't need to end your marriage first.

Immigration requirements for people subject to immigration controls

The civil partnerships provisions for people subject to immigration control are exactly the same as those in place for marriage. These apply if one partner is a non-EEA (European Immigration Area) citizen and is subject to immigration control, for example in the UK on a visa.

People subject to immigration control who want to give notice of a civil partnership need to do so at a register office designated for this purpose. They are required to produce one of the following as part of that notice:

• entry clearance granted to form a civil partnership

- A Home Office certificate of approval
- Indefinite leave to remain in the UK.

Registrars are required to report any civil partnerships to the immigration service if they have any suspicions.

Application for leave to remain

Civil partners of British citizens and people settled here can apply for an initial period of two years leave to remain in the UK. If they are still together at the end of that period they can apply for indefinite leave to remain.

Work permit holders and students

Civil partners of people with temporary leave to remain in the UK, such as students and work permit holders, can apply for leave along with their civil partners.

A list of Register Offices for people subject to immigration control, can be found at:

www.gov.uk/government/organisations/uk-visas-and-immigration.

Civil partnership registration for two non-EAA citizens

Two non-EAA citizens can register a civil partnership together in the UK as long as they have entry clearance for the purpose of doing so and have resided in the registration district for at least seven days before giving notice. Registering a civil partnership doesn't affect their immigration status.

Registering civil partnerships abroad

If couples wish to register a civil partnership abroad they should contact the Embassy or High Commission in the country concerned. Couples may be asked to obtain a certificate of no impediment.

It may be possible for couples to register at a UK consulate in another country if one of them is a UK national. However, UK consulates will not register civil partnerships if the host country objects or if civil unions or same sex marriage is available in that country.

Armed Forces

Members of the Armed Forces can register civil partnerships overseas in those areas where a Servicing Registering Officer is able to offer this service.

Overseas relationships

It may be the case that a couple has formed a civil union, registered partnership, domestic partnership or same-sex marriage abroad. Couples in those kind of relationships can automatically be recognised in the UK as civil partners without having to register again provided conditions set out in sections 212 to 218 of the Civil Partnership Act are met.

The legislation defines an overseas relationship that can be treated as a civil partnership in the UK as one that is either specified in Schedule 20 to the Civil Partnership Act or one which meets general conditions in the Act and certain other conditions.

Schedule 20 of the Act lists countries and relationships that are recognised.

However, since section 20 was enacted many more countries (50 to date) bringing the total up to 75, have enacted laws to enable civil partnerships and gay marriage. For an up to date list you should go to Civil Partnership Act 2004 (Overseas Relationships) Order 2012. This amends schedule 20.

A couple who have formed a relationship recognised in one of those countries can be recognised in the UK as civil partners if they are of the same sex, the relationship has been registered with a responsible body in that country, the couple were eligible to enter into a civil relationship in that country and all procedural requirements have been fulfilled.

For foreign relationships in countries not listed in the amended Schedule 20 a couple who have formed a relationship can still be recognised as civil partners if the foreign relationship meets the general conditions set out in the Civil Partnerships Act.

Dissolution of relationships formed abroad

Where a couple have formed an overseas relationship and that relationship is treated as a civil partnership in the UK, they may be able to obtain a dissolution, annulment or legal separation here. Legal advice should be sought in this matter.

Family relationships

The law now recognises the role of both civil partners in respect of a child living in their household.

Adoption

Under the Adoption and Children Act 2002, which came into force on 30th December 2005, civil partners may apply jointly to adopt a child.

Parental responsibility

Under the Adoption and Children Act 2002, a person will also be able to acquire parental responsibility for the child of their civil partner. They can do this with the agreement of their civil partner. If the child's other parent also has parental responsibility, both parents must agree. Parental responsibility can also be acquired on application to the court. Civil partners will have a duty to provide maintenance for each other and any children of the civil partnership.

Social security, tax credits and child support

Entering into a civil partnership will affect entitlements to the benefits and tax credits a person may be receiving. From 5th December 2005, the income of a civil partner has been taken into account when calculating entitlement to income related benefits. These benefits include income support, income based job seekers allowance, pension credit, housing benefit and council tax benefit. For more advice concerning benefits you should go to citizensadvice.org.uk.

From 5th December the income of a civil partner has been taken into account when calculating entitlement to child and working tax credits. The Tax Credit Line on 0345 300 3900 can offer further advice.

Child support

From 5th December 2005, civil partners who are parents will be treated in the same way as married partners for child support. Also, parents who are living with a same sex partner even where they have not formed a civil partnership will be treated in the same way as parents who live together with an opposite sex partner but who are not married. For further information contact the Child Support

on 1 800 840 8757.

Pensions

Survivor benefits in occupational and personal pension schemes. Surviving civil partners will be entitled to a pension based on accrued pension right. New rules for civil partners mean that a surviving partner will benefit from a survivors pension based on the contracted out pension rights accrued by their deceased partner from 1988 to the date of retirement or death if this occurs before retirement. This new rule applies to all contracted out private pension schemes.

State pensions

From 5th December 2005, civil partners have enjoyed most of the same state pension rights as husbands and they will treated the same as husbands and wives after 2010 when the treatment of men and women will be equalised. For more information concerning pensions contact the Pensions Advisory Service on 0800 011 3797.

Tax

From 5th December 2005, civil partners have been treated the same as married couples for tax purposes. Information is available from a local tax office and the HMRC website www.hmrc.gov.uk

Employment rights

Employers are required to treat both married partners and civil partners in the same way. The Employment Equality (Sexual Orientation) Regulations 2003 have been amended to ensure that civil partners receive the same treatment and can bring a claim for sexual orientation discrimination if this is not the case. Other areas where changes are made include flexible working, where a civil partner of a child under six or disabled child under 18 will be able to take advantage of flexible working arrangements. Paternity and adoption leave will now be the right of civil partners More information on paternity and adoption leave and pay can be found on www.moneyadviceservice.org.uk.

Wills

Like all people, couples or not, making a will is the most sensible way of ensuring equitable disposal of your assets in accordance with your wishes. The most valuable asset is usually a home and this will automatically vest in a civil partner after death of the other partner, whether or not a will expressly states this. All other property belonging to one of the civil partners will be disposed of according to the will. If a person has a will and then registers a civil partnership it will be revoked automatically unless it expressly states otherwise. If a person dies without making a will there are special legal rules which determine how the estate of the deceased should be shared amongst that persons relatives.

Where a person is married or in a civil partnership and has no other surviving close relatives

Where a person dies intestate and leaves a spouse or civil partner who survives the deceased by at least 28 days and the deceased has no surviving children, parents, brothers or sisters or nieces or nephews (half brothers, sisters, nieces and nephews are not included) then the whole of the deceased's estate goes to the surviving spouse or civil partner.

Where a person is married or in a civil partnership and has no children but leaves other surviving close relatives

If the deceased has no children at the time of his or her death but leaves a parent or a brother or sister or a niece or nephew (again half brothers, sisters, nieces and nephews are not included) then the spouse or civil partner will inherit the personal possessions of the deceased plus the first £450,000 of the deceased's estate.

The spouse or civil partner will also receive half of the balance of the deceased's assets over £450,000. The remaining half passes to the deceased's parents, or if he or she has no surviving parents, to his or her brothers and sisters. If the deceased has no surviving parents to brothers and sisters the remaining half passes to any surviving nieces and nephews.

Where a person is married or in a civil partnership and leaves children

If the deceased leaves a child or children the surviving spouse or civil partner will inherit the deceased's personal possessions plus the first £250,000 of the deceased's estate. The spouse or civil partner has a right to receive an income from half of the balance of the deceased's estate over £250,000. The remaining half of the balance passes to the deceased's children when they reach the age of 18 or to the deceased's grandchildren if his or her own children die before him or her. When the spouse or civil partner of the deceased dies the first half of the balance also passes to the children.

Separated and divorced spouses

Where the deceased and his or her spouse or civil partner have been judicially separated the former spouse or civil partner does not inherit anything. Similarly, where a couple have been divorced or a civil partnership has been dissolved the surviving spouse or civil partner does not inherit anything.

Not married or in a civil partnership and leaves children

Where a person dies intestate and does not leave a spouse or civil partner (or where the spouse or civil dies within 28 days of the deceased) and the deceased has children then the whole of the deceased's estate goes to his or her surviving children.

Person is not married/in a civil partnership and has no children

Where a person dies intestate and does not leave a spouse or civil partner (or where the spouse or civil dies within 28 days of the deceased) and the deceased does not have any children then the whole of the deceased's estate goes to his or her surviving parents (step-parents and in-laws are excluded) in equal shares.

If the deceased has no surviving partner, children or parents then the whole of his or her estate will be inherited by the deceased's brothers and sisters (half-brothers and sisters are excluded). If there are no brothers or sisters the deceased's estate passes to any half-brothers and sisters. If there are no half-brothers and sisters the estate passes to the deceased's grandparents.

If there are no surviving grandparents it passes to the deceased's uncles and aunts and if there are no surviving uncles and aunts it passes to any half-uncles and aunts.

Where a person dies leaving no surviving close relatives

Where a person dies leaving no surviving spouse or civil partner, no children, siblings or grandchildren and no aunts or uncles the deceased's estate passes to the Crown or the Duchy of Lancaster or the Duke of Cornwall.

The role of the courts

The Courts have the power to override the rules of intestacy where the distribution of a person's estate in accordance with the rules would not adequately provide for family members in certain circumstances.

Life assurance

Civil partners can hold life insurance on their partner's life on the same basis as a married person. In the event of an accident caused by negligence of another then the civil partner can claim compensation and can claim bereavement damages, currently £15120 (from May 2020). Similarly, someone living with the deceased as though they had been in a civil partnership for two years prior to date of death will also be entitled to claim compensation as a dependant.

Tenancy rights

The general effect of the Civil Partnerships Act has been to give the same rights to civil partners as married couples. The Act also equalises the rights of same sex couples who are living together as if they were civil partners and their families with those of unmarried opposite sex couples.

Private sector tenants

The same sex partner of an assured tenant or assured shorthold tenant will have the same rights of succession to a tenancy as those tenants of local authority or registered social landlords. For further information on housing and tenancies visit www.gov.uk

****

Chapter 4.

Dissolution of Civil Partnerships

The rules for dissolution of a civil partnership are different for Scotland and Northern Ireland. For the rules in Scotland go to: www.scotcourts.gov.uk/taking-action/divorce-and-dissolution-of-civil-partnership For northern Ireland go to:

www.nidirect.gov.uk/articles/getting-divorcedissolution-civil-partnership

Dissolution of a Civil Partnership, Nullity and Other Proceedings.

Paragraph 34 of the Marriage (Same Sex Persons) Act 2013 amends the provisions in the Civil partnership Act, which set out how a civil partnership can be ended. The amendment provides that, in addition to death, dissolution and annulment, a civil partnership ends if it is converted into a marriage under section 9 of the Act. Section 37 of Chapter 2 of the Civil Partnerships Act 2004 deals with the ending of a civil partnership, either through dissolution or nullity or other.

As with marriage, problems may arise and partners to a civil partnership may wish to terminate the union. Likewise, the union may not, for some reason, be legal and may be annulled.

Later chapters deal with economic and other matters which will arise after dissolution.

By virtue of Section 37 the court may:

a) make a dissolution order which dissolves a civil partnership on the ground that it has broken down irretrievably;

b) make a nullity order which annuls a civil partnership which is void or voidable;

c) make a presumption of death order which dissolves a civil partnership on the ground that one of the civil partners is presumed to be dead;

d) make a separation order which provides for the separation of the civil partners.

Further, every dissolution, nullity or presumption of death order:

a) is, in the first instance, a conditional order and;

b) may not be made final before the end of the prescribed period (see below).

A nullity order made where a civil partnership is voidable annuls the civil partnership only as respects any time after the order, and the civil partnership is to be treated (despite the order) as if it had existed up to that time. Courts can be the High Court or, if the County Court has jurisdiction by virtue of Part 5 of the Matrimonial and Family Proceedings Act 1984, a county court.

74

The period before conditional orders can be made final

Section 38 of the Act states that the prescribed period referred to above is:

a) 6 weeks from the making of the conditional order, or

b) if the 6-week period would end on a day on which the office or the registry dealing with the case is closed, the period of 6 weeks extended to the first day on which the offices are next open.

This prescribed period can be replaced with a different definition by the Lord Chancellor. Six months, however, will be the maximum prescribed period. In a particular case, the court dealing with the case can shorten the prescribed period. Any instrument carrying such an order is subject to annulment by a resolution of either houses of parliament.

Intervention of the Queen's proctor

This section, 39, will apply if an application has been made for a dissolution, nullity or presumption of death order. The court may, if it thinks fit, direct all necessary papers are to be sent to the Queen's proctor who must under the directions of the Attorney General instruct counsel to argue before the court any question in relation to the matter which the court considers it necessary or expedient to have fully argued.

If any person at any time either during the progress of the proceedings or before the conditional order is made final gives information to the Queen's Proctor on any matter material to the due decision of the case, the Queen's proctor may take such steps as the Attorney general considers necessary or expedient.

If the Queen's Proctor does intervene the courts can award costs of such an intervention against appropriate parties.

Proceedings before an order has been made final

Section 40 deals with any proceedings or events prior to an order being made final. The section applies if a conditional order has been made and the Queen's proctor or any other person who has not been party to a proceedings in which an order was made, shows cause why the order should not be made final on the ground that material facts have not been brought before the court. The section also applies if:

a) a conditional order has been made,

b) three months have elapsed since the earliest date on which an application could have been made for the order to be made final,

c) no such application has been made by the civil partner who applied for the conditional order, and

d) the other civil partner makes an application to the court under this section.

The court may:

a) make the order final

b) rescind the order

c) require further enquiry

d) other wise deal with the case as it thinks fit.

Time bar on application for dissolution orders

Section 41 of the Act deals with time limits on applications for orders. No application for a dissolution order may be made to the court before the end of the period of one year from the formation of the civil partnership. Nothing in the section prevents an application being made which includes matters that happened before the end of the 1-year period.

Attempts at reconciliation of civil partners

Section 42 of the Act applies where an application has been made for a dissolution or separation order. The rules of the court must make provision for requiring the solicitor acting for the applicant to certify whether he or she has discussed with the applicant the possibility of a reconciliation with the civil partner and given the applicant the name and address of persons qualified to act in helping to effect a reconciliation of the civil partners. If at any stage of the proceedings it seems to the court that there is a reasonable possibility of a reconciliation between the civil partners, the court may adjourn the proceedings for such period as it thinks fit to enable attempts to be made to effect a reconciliation between them.

Consideration by the court of any agreements or arrangements

Section 43 applies in cases where proceedings for a dissolution or separation order is contemplated or have begun and an agreement or arrangement is made or proposed to be made between the civil partners which relates to, arises out of, or is connected with, the proceedings. The civil partners, or either of them, can refer the arrangement to court and the court will consider the arrangement.

Dissolution of a civil partnership which has broken down irretrievably

Subject to section 41, under section 44 of the Act, an application for a dissolution order may be made to the court by either civil partner on the ground that the civil partnership has broken down irretrievably. On an application for a dissolution order the court must inquire, as far as it reasonably can, into:

a) the facts alleged by the applicant, and
b) the facts alleged by the respondent.

The court hearing an application for a dissolution order must not hold that the civil partnership has broken down irretrievably unless the applicant satisfies the court of one or more of the facts described below (sub section 5(a), (b), (c) or (d)). If the court is satisfied of any of the facts described below it must make a dissolution order unless it is satisfied on all the evidence that the partnership has not broken down irretrievably.

The facts laid out in subsection 5(a) (b) (c) or (d) of section 41 of the act are:

a) that the respondent has behaved in such a way that the applicant cannot reasonably be expected to live with the respondent;

b) that:

    (i)   the applicant and the respondent have lived apart for a continuous period of at least 2 years immediately preceding the making of the application (2 years separation), and

    (ii)   the respondent consents to a dissolution order being made;

c) that the applicant and the respondent have lived apart for a continuous period of at least 5 years immediately preceding the making of the application (5 years separation);

d) that the respondent has deserted the applicant for a continuous period of at least 2 years immediately preceding the making of the application.

Supplemental provisions as to facts raising presumption of breakdown

Section 45 of the Act relates to additional facts that effect the making of an order for a dissolution of a civil partnership.

a) in any proceedings for a dissolution order the applicant alleges, in reliance on s44 (5)(a) that the respondent has behaved in such a way that the applicant cannot reasonably be expected to live with the respondent, but

b) after the date of the occurrence of the final incident relied on by the applicant and held by the court to support his allegation, the applicant and the respondent have lived together for a period (or period) which does not, or which taken together do not, exceed 6 months.

The fact that the applicant and respondent have lived together as mentioned in subsection (b) must be disregarded in determining, for the purposes of 44(5)(b) whether the applicant cannot reasonably be expected to live with the respondent.

Section 45 states that the rules of the court must make provision for the purpose of ensuring that the respondent has been given such information as will enable him or her to understand the consequences to him of consenting to the making of the order and the steps which he or she must take to indicate consent.

For the purposes of section 44(5)(d) the court may treat a period of desertion as having continued at a time when the deserting partner was incapable of continuing the necessary intention, if the evidence before the court is such that, had he not been so incapable, the court would have inferred that the desertion would have continued at that time.

In considering for the purposes of section 44(5) whether the period for which the civil partners have lived apart or the period for which the respondent has deserted the applicant has been continuous, no account is to be taken of :

a) any one period not exceeding 6 months, or
b) any two or more periods no exceeding 6 months in all, during which the civil partners resumed living with each other.

But no period during which the civil partners have lived with each other counts as part of the period during which the civil partners have lived apart as part of the period of desertion.

Dissolution order not precluded by previous separation order etc

Section 46 of the Act states that subsections (1) (2) and (3) apply if any of the following orders has been made in relation to a civil partnership:

a) a separation order;
b) an order under schedule 6 to the Act (financial relief in magistrates courts etc)
c) an order under section 33 of the Family Law Act 1966 (c.27) (occupation orders)
d) an order under section 37 of the 1996 Act (orders where neither civil partner entitled to share the home)

Subsection (2) states that nothing prevents either civil partner from applying for a dissolution order or the court from making a dissolution order on the same facts, or substantially the same facts, as those proved in support of the making of the order referred to above.

Subsection (3) section 46 states that on the application for the dissolution order the court may treat the order referred to above as sufficient proof of any desertion or other fact by reference to which it was made but must not make the dissolution order without receiving evidence from the applicant.

Subsection (4) states that if the application for the dissolution order follows a separation order or any order requiring the civil partners to live apart, and there was a degree of desertion immediately preceding the institution of the proceedings for the separation order, and the civil partners have not resumed living together and the separation order has continuously been in force since it was made, then the period of desertion is to be treated for the purposes of the application of the dissolution order as if it had immediately preceded the making of the application.

Subsection (5) states that for the purposes of s (44)(5)(d) the court may treat as a period during which the respondent has deserted the applicant any period during which there was in force:

a) an injunction granted by the high court or a county court which excludes the respondent from the civil partnership home, or

b) an order under section 33 or 37 of the 1996 Act which prohibits the respondent from occupying a dwelling house in which the applicant and the respondent have or at any time have had, a civil partnership home.

Refusal of dissolution in 5-year separation cases on grounds of grave hardship

Section 47 deals with the opposing of a dissolution order by the respondent. Subsection (1) states that the respondent to an application for a dissolution order in which the applicant alleges 5 years separation may oppose the making of the order on the grounds that:

a) the dissolution of the civil partnership will result in grave or other financial hardship to him/her, and,

b) it would in all the circumstances be wrong to dissolve the civil partnership.

Subsection (2) states that subsection (3) (below) applies if:

a) the making of a dissolution order is opposed under this section,

b) the court finds that the applicant is entitled to rely in support of his application on the fact of 5 years separation and makes no such finding as to any other fact mentioned in section 44(5), and

c) apart from this section, the court would make a dissolution order.

Subsection 3 states that the court must consider all the circumstances, including the conduct of the civil partners and the interests of the civil partners and any of the children or other persons concerned, and if it is of the opinion that the ground mentioned in subsection 1 is made out, dismiss the application for the dissolution order.

Subsection (4) further defines 'hardship' as including the loss of the chance of acquiring any benefit which the respondent might acquire if the civil partnership were not dissolved.

Proceedings before order made final: protection for respondent in separation cases

Section 48 of the Act deals with the protection of the respondent in separation cases. Subsection (1) states that the court may, on application made by the respondent, rescind a conditional dissolution order if:

a) it made the order on the basis of a finding that the applicant was entitled to rely on the fact of 2 years separation coupled with the respondents consent to a dissolution order being made,

b) it made no such finding as to any other fact mentioned in section 44(5) and

c) it is satisfied that the applicant misled the respondent (whether intentionally or unintentionally) about any matter which the respondent took into account when deciding to give his consent.

Subsection 2 of section 48 states that subsections (3) to (5) apply if:

a) the respondent to an application for a dissolution order in which the applicant alleged:

    (i)   2 years separation coupled with the respondent's consent to a dissolution order being made, or

    (ii)   5 years separation

    (iii)   has applied to the court for consideration under subsection (3) of his financial position after the dissolution of the civil partnership, and

b) the court:

    (i)   has made a conditional dissolution order on the basis of a finding that the applicant was entitled to rely in support of his application on the fact of 2 years or 5 years separation, and

    (ii)   has made no such finding as to any other fact mentioned in section 44(5).

    (iii)   Subsection (3) of section 48 states that the court hearing an application by the respondent under subsection (2) must consider all the circumstances, including:

a) the health, age, conduct, earning capacity, financial resources and financial obligations of each of the parties, and

b) the financial position of the respondent as, having regard to the dissolution it is likely to be after the death of the applicant should the applicant die first.

c) Subsection (4) states that, subject to subsection (5) the court must not make an order final unless it is satisfied that:

a) the applicant should not be required to make any financial provision for the respondent, or

b) the financial provision made by the applicant for the respondent is-

(i)   fair and reasonable

(ii)   the best that can be made in the circumstances.

Subsection (5) states that the court may if it thinks fit make the order final if:

a) it appears that there are circumstances making it desirable that the order should be made final without delay, and

b) it has obtained a satisfactory undertaking from the applicant that he will make such financial provision for the respondent as it may approve.

Nullity

Grounds on which a civil partnership is void

Section 49 deals with nullity of a civil partnership. Nullity effectively means a void civil partnership.

Where two people register as civil partners of each other in England and Wales, the civil partnership is void if:

a) at the time when they do so, they are not eligible to register as civil partners under Chapter 1,

b) at the time when they do so they both know-

    (i)   that the notice of proposed civil partnership has not been given,

    (ii)   that the civil partnership document has not been duly issued,

    (iii)   that the civil partnership document is void

    (iv)   that the place of registration is a place other than that specified in the notices (or notice) of proposed civil partnership and the civil partnership document, or

(v)   that a civil partnership registrar is not present, or

(vi)   the civil partnership document is void under paragraph 6 (5) of Schedule 2 to the Act (civil partnership between child and another person forbidden). .

Grounds on which civil partnership is voidable

Section 50 of the Act deals with grounds on which a civil partnership can be voided. Subsection (1) states that where two people register as civil partners of each other in England and Wales, the civil partnership is voidable if:

a) either of them did not validly consent to its formation (whether as a result of duress, mistake, unsoundness of mind or otherwise)

b) at the time of its formation either of them, though capable of giving a valid consent, was suffering, whether continuously or intermittently, from mental disorder of such a kind or to such an extent as to be unfitted for civil partnership;

c) at the time of its formation, the respondent was pregnant by some person other than the applicant;

d) an interim gender recognition certificate under the Gender Recognition Act 2004 (c.7) has, after the time of its formation, been issued to either civil partner;

e) the respondent is a person whose gender at the time of its formation had become the acquired gender under the 2004 Act.

f) (2) In this section and section 51 'mental disorder' has the same meaning as in the Mental Health Act 1983 (c.20).

Bars to relief where civil partnership is voidable

Section 51 deals with relief in relation to making a nullity order. Subsection (1) of section 51 states that the court must not make a nullity order on the ground that a civil partnership is voidable if the respondent satisfies the court:

a) that the applicant, with knowledge that it was open to him to obtain a nullity order, conducted himself in relation to the respondent in such a way as to lead the respondent reasonably to believe that he would not seek to do so, and

b) that it would be unjust to the respondent to make the order.

Subsection 2 states that, without prejudice to subsection (1) the court must not make a nullity order by virtue of section 50(1)(a),(b)(C) or(e) unless-

a) it is satisfied that proceedings were instituted within 3 years from the date of the formation of the civil partnership, or

b) leave for the institution of proceedings after the end of that 3 year period has been granted under subsection (3).

Subsection (3) states that a judge of the court may, on an application made to him, grant leave for the intention of proceedings if he:

a) is satisfied that the applicant has at some time during the three year period suffered from mental disorder, and

b) considers that in all the circumstances of the case it would be just to grant leave for the institution of the proceedings.

Subsection (4) states that an application for leave under subsection (3) may be made after the end of the 3 year period.

Subsection (5) states that, without prejudice to subsection (1) the court must not make a nullity order by virtue of section 50(1)(d) unless it is satisfied that proceedings were instituted within the period of 6 months from the date of issue of the interim gender recognition certificate.

Subsection (6) states that, without prejudice to subsection (1) and (2) the court must not make a nullity order by virtue of section 50(1)(c) or (e) unless it is satisfied that the applicant was at the time of the formation of the civil partnership ignorant of the facts alleged.

Proof of certain matters not necessary to validity of civil partnership

Section 52, subsection (1) of the Act states that where two people have registered as civil partners of each other in England and Wales, it is not necessary in support of the civil partnership to give any proof:

a) that any person whose consent to the civil partnership was required under section 4 (parental etc. consent) had given his consent, or

b) that the civil partnership registrar was designated as such by the registration authority in whose area the registration took place;

and no evidence is to be given to prove the contrary in any proceedings touching the validity of the civil partnership.

Power to validate civil partnership

Section 53 of the Act deals with powers to validate a civil partnership. Subsection (1) of section 53 states that where two people have registered as civil partners of each other in England and Wales, the Lord Chancellor may by order validate the civil partnership if it appears to him that it is or may be void under section 49(b).

Subsection (2) states that an order under subsection (1) may include provisions for relieving a person from any liability under section 31(2) 32(2) Or 33(5) or (7).

Subsection (3) states that the draft of an order under subsection (1) must be advertised, in such manner as the Lord Chancellor thinks fit, not less than one month before the order is made.

Subsection (4) states that the Lord Chancellor must:

a) consider all objections to the order sent to him in writing during that month, and

b) if it appears to him necessary, direct a local enquiry into the validity of any such objections.

Subsection (5) states that an order under subsection (1) is subject to special parliamentary procedure.

Validity of civil partnerships registered outside England and Wales

Section 54 of the Act deals with civil partnerships registered outside England and Wales. Subsection (1) of section 54 states that where two people register as civil partners of each other in Scotland, the civil partnership is-

Subsection (2) states that where two people register as civil partners of each other in Northern Ireland, the civil partnership is-

a) void, if it would be void in Northern Ireland under section 173, and

b) voidable, if circumstances fall within any paragraph of section 50(1).

1. Subsection (3) states that subsection (4) below applies where two people register as civil partners of each other under an order in Council under-

2. section 210 (registration at British consulates etc,) or

3. section 211 (registration by armed forces personnel),

(the 'relevant section')

Subsection (4) states that the civil partnership is-

a) void, if-

    (i)   the condition in subsection (2) (a) Or (b) of the relevant section is not met, or

    (ii)   a requirement prescribed for the purposes of this paragraph by an Order in Council under the relevant section is not complied with, and

        (b) voidable if,

Subsection (5) states that the appropriate part of the United kingdom is the part by reference to which the condition in subsection (2)(b) of the relevant section is met.

Subsection (6) states that subsections (7) and (8) below apply where two people have registered an apparent or alleged overseas relationship.

(7) The civil partnership is void if-

a) the relationship is not an overseas relationship, or

b) (even though the relationship is an overseas relationship) the parties are not treated under chapter 2 of part 5 as having formed a civil partnership.

(8) The civil partnership is voidable if-

a) the overseas relationship is voidable under section 50(1)(d), or

b) the circumstances fall within section 50(1)(d), or

c) where either of the parties was domiciled in England and Wales or Northern Ireland at the time when the overseas relationship was registered, the circumstances fall within section 50(1)(a)(b)(c)or(e)

Presumption of death orders

Section 55 of the Act deals with presumption of death orders. Subsection (1) states that the court may, on an application made by a civil partner, make a presumption of death order if it is

94

satisfied that reasonable grounds exist for supposing that the other civil partner is dead.

Subsection (2) states that, in any proceedings under this section the fact that:

a) for a period of 7 years or more the civil partner has been continually absent from the applicant, and

b) the applicant has no reason to believe that the other civil partner has been living within that time.

is evidence that the other civil partner is dead until the contrary is proved.

Separation orders

Section 56 deals with separation orders. Subsection (1) of section 56 states that an application for a separation order may be made to the court by either civil partner on the ground that any such fact as is mentioned in section 44(5)(a),(b),(c) or (d) exists.

Subsection (2) states that on an application for a separation order the court must inquire, so far as it reasonably can, into-

a) the facts alleged by the applicant, and

b) any facts alleged by the respondent,

but whether the civil partnership has broken down irretrievably is irrelevant.

Subsection (3) states that, if the court is satisfied on the evidence of any such fact as mentioned in section 44(5)(a),(b),(c) or (d) it must, subject to section 63, make a separation order.

Subsection (4) states that section 45 (supplemental provisions as to facts raising presumption of breakdown) applies for the purposes of an application for a separation order alleging any such fact as it applies in relation to an application for a dissolution order alleging that fact.

Effect of a separation order

Section 57 deals with the effect of a separation order. If either civil partner dies intestate as respects all or any of his or her real or personal property while a separation order is in force and the separation is continuing, the property as respects which he or she died intestate devolves as if the other civil partner had then been dead.

Declarations

Section 58 of the Act deals with declarations. Subsection (1) of section 58 states that any person may apply to the high court or a county court for one or more of the following declarations in relation to a civil partnership specified in the application:

a) a declaration that the civil partnership was at its inception a valid civil partnership;

b) a declaration that the civil partnership subsisted on a date specified in the application;

c) a declaration that the civil partnership did not subsist on a date so specified;

d) a declaration that the validity of a dissolution, annulment or legal separation obtained outside England and Wales in respect of the civil partnership is entitled to recognition in England and Wales;

e) a declaration that the validity of a dissolution, annulment or legal separation so obtained in respect of the civil partnership is not entitled to recognition in England and Wales.

Subsection (2) of section 58 states that where an application under subsection (1) is made to a court by a person other than a civil partner in the civil partnership to which the application relates, the court must refuse to hear the application if it considers that the applicant does not have a sufficient interest in the determination of that application.

General provisions as to making and effect of declarations

Section 59 of the Act deals with general provisions relating to the making and effect of declarations. Subsection (1) of section 59 states that where on an application for a declaration under section 58 the truth of the proposition to be declared is proved to the satisfaction of the court, the court must make the declaration unless to do so would be manifestly contrary to public policy.

Subsection (2) states that ay declaration under section 58 binds her majesty and all other persons.

Subsection (3) states that the court, on the dismissal of an application for a declaration under section 58, may not make any declaration for which an application has not been made.

Subsection (4) states that no declaration which may be applied for under section 58 may be made otherwise than under section 58 by any court.

Subsection (5) states that no declaration may be made by any court, whether under section 58 or otherwise, that a civil partnership was, at its inception void.

Subsection (6) states that nothing in this section affects the powers of any court to make a nullity order in respect of a civil partnership.

The Attorney General and proceedings for declarations

Section 60 of the Act deals with the powers of the Attorney General to intervene with an application under section 58 and also the powers of the court to refer a matter to him or her.

Supplementary provisions as to declarations

Section 61 deals with supplementary provisions relating to declarations. Subsection (1) of section 61 of the Act states that any declaration made under section 68, and any application for such a declaration, must be in the form prescribed by the rules of the court. Subsection (2) states that the rules of the court may make provision as to the information required to be given by any applicant for a declaration under section 58. The rules can also require notice of an application under section 58 to be served on the attorney general and on persons who may be affected by any declaration applied for.

Subsection (3) states that no proceedings under section 58 affect any final judgement or order already pronounced or made by any court of competent jurisdiction. Subsection (4) states that the court hearing an application under section 58 may direct that the whole or part of any proceedings must be heard in private.

Subsection (5) states that an application for a direction under subsection (4) must be heard in private unless the court other wise directs.

General provisions under Chapter two of the Act

Sections 62 63 and 64 deal with general provisions. Section 62 deals with relief for respondents in dissolution proceedings, Section 63 deals with restrictions on making of orders affecting children (the court must consider the effects of any dissolution, nullity or separation orders on the welfare of children). Subsection (1) of section 63 states that in any proceedings for a dissolution, nullity or separation order, the court must consider:

a) whether there are any children of the family to whom this section applies, and

b) if thee are any such children, whether (in the light of the arrangements which have been, or are proposed to be, made for their upbringing and welfare) it should exercise any of its powers under the Children Act 1989 (c.41) with respect to any of them.

Subsection (2) states that, if, in the case of any child to whom this section applies, it appears to the court that-

a) the circumstances of the case require it, or are likely to require it, to exercise any of its powers under the 1989 Act with respect to any such child,

b) it is not in the position to exercise the power or (as the case may be) those powers without giving further consideration to the case, and

c) there are exceptional circumstances which make it desirable in the interests of the child that the court should give a direction under this section, it may direct that the order is not to be made final, or (in the case of a separation order) is not to be made, until the court orders otherwise.

Subsection (3) states that this section applies to:

a) any child of the family who has not reached 16 at the date when the court considers the case in accordance with the requirements of this section, and

b) any child of the family who has reached 16 at that date and in relation to whom the court directs that this section shall apply.

Section 64 deals with general rules concerning parties to proceedings under Chapter 2 of the act.

In the next chapter, we will look at Civil Partnerships and property and financial arrangements

****

Chapter 5.

Property and Financial Arrangements

Property and Financial Arrangements

Section 65 of Chapter 3 of the 2004 Civil Partnerships Act deals with property and financial arrangements in relation to entitlements generally and the event of a dissolution and ending of a partnership.

Subsection (1) of section 65 applies if:

a) a civil partner contributes in money or money's worth to the improvement of real or personal property in which or in the proceeds of sale of which either or both of the civil partners has or have a beneficial interest, and

b) the contribution is of a substantial nature.

Subsection (2) states that the contributing partner is to be treated as having acquired by virtue of the contribution a share or an enlarged share (as the case may be) in the beneficial interest of such an extent:

a) as may have been then agreed, or

b) in default of such agreement, as may seem in all the circumstances just to any court before which the question of the existence or extent of the beneficial interest of either civil partners arises (whether in proceedings between them or in any other proceedings)

Subsection (3) states that subsection (2) is subject to any agreement (express or implied) between the civil partners to the contrary.

Disputes between civil partners about property

Section 66 of the Act deals with disputes about property. Subsection (1) of section 66 states that in any question between the civil partners in a civil partnership as to title to or possession of property, either civil partner may apply to the High Court or such county court as may be prescribed by rules of court.

Subsection (2) states that on such an application, the court may make such order with respect to the property as it thinks fit (including an order for the sale of the property).

Subsection (3) states that rules of the court made for the purpose of this section may confer jurisdiction on county courts whatever the situation or value of the property in dispute.

Applications under section 66 where property not in possession etc.

Section 67 deals with applications under section 66 where one or other civil partner has property which is in possession of one person only.

Subsection (1) of section 67 states that the right of a civil partner (A) to make an application under section 66 includes the right to make such an application where A claims that the other civil partner (B) has had in his possession or under his control:

a) money to which, or to a share of which, A was beneficially entitled, or

b) property (other than money) to which, or to an interest in which, A was beneficially entitled, and that either the money or other property has ceased to be in B's possession or under B's control or that A does not know whether it is still in B's possession or under B's control.

Subsection (2) states that for the purposes of subsection (1)(a) it does not matter whether A is beneficially entitled to the money or share: because it represents the proceeds of the property to which, or to an interest in which, A was beneficially entitled, or

a)   for any other reason.

Subsection (3) states that subsections (4) and (5) below apply if, on such an application being made, the court is satisfied that B:

a) has had in his possession or under his control money or other property as mentioned in subsection (1)(a) or (b), and

b) has not made to A, in respect of that money or other property, such payment or disposition as would have been appropriate in the circumstances.

Subsection (4) states that the power of the court to make orders under section 66 includes power to order B to pay A:

a) in a case falling within subsection (1)(a) such sum in respect of the money to which the application relates, or A's share of it, the court considers appropriate, or

b) in a case falling within subsection (1)(b), such sum in respect of the value of the property to which the application relates, or A's interest in it, as the court considers appropriate.

Subsection (5) states that if it appears to the court that there is any property which:

a) represents the whole or the part of the money or property, and

b) is property in respect of which an order could (apart from this section) have been made under section 66, the court may (either instead of or as well as making an order in accordance with subsection (4) make any order which it could (apart from this section) have made under section 66.

Subsection (6) states that any power of the court which is exercisable on an application under section 66 is exercisable in relation to an application made under that section as extended by that section.

Applications under section 66 by former civil partners

Section 68 of the Act deals with applications by former civil partners. Subsection (1) of section 68 states that this section applies where a civil partnership has been dissolved or annulled. Subsection (2) states that, subject to subsection (3) below, an application may be made under section 66 (including that section as extended by section 67) by either former civil partner despite the dissolution or annulment (and references in those sections to a civil partner are to be read accordingly).

Subsection (3) states that the application must be made within the period of 3 years beginning with the date of the dissolution or annulment.

Actions in tort between civil partners

Section 69 of the Act deals with tortuous actions between civil partners. Subsection (1) of section 69 states that this section applies if an action in tort is brought by one civil partner against the other during the subsistence of the civil partnership.

Subsection (2) states that the court may stay the proceedings if it appears:

a) that no substantial benefit would accrue to either civil partner from the continuation of the proceedings, or

b) that the question or questions in issue could more conveniently be disposed of on an application under section 66.

Subsection (3) states that without prejudice to subsection (2)(b) the court may in such an action-

a) exercise any power which could be exercised on an application under section 66, or

b) give such direction as it thinks fit for the disposal under that section of any question arising in the proceedings.

Assurance policy by civil partner for benefit of other civil partner etc.

Section 70 of the Act deals with above policies of assurance. Section 11 of the Married Women's Property Act 1882 (c.75) (money paid under policy of insurance not to form part of the estate of the insured) applies in relation to a policy of assurance:

a) effected by a civil partner on his own life, and

b) expressed to be for the benefit of his civil partner, or of his children, or of his civil partner and children, or any of them, as it applies in relation to a policy of assurance effected by a husband and expressed to be for the benefit of his wife, or of his children, or of his wife and children, or of any of them.

Wills, administration of estates and family provision

Section 71 deals with wills and estates administration and states that schedule 4 to the Act amends enactments relating to wills, administration of estates and family provisions so that they apply in civil partnerships as they apply to marriages.

Financial relief for civil partners and children of the family

Section 72 of the Act deals with financial relief during a proceedings to end a civil partnership. Subsection (1) of section 72 states that Schedule 5 to the Act makes provision for financial relief in connection with civil partnerships that corresponds to provision made for financial relief in connection with marriages by part 2 of the Matrimonial Causes Act 1973 (c.18).

Subsection (2) states that any rule of law under which any provision of Part 2 of the 1973 Act is interpreted as applying to dissolution of a marriage on the ground of presumed death is to be treated as applying (with any necessary modifications) in relation to the corresponding provision of Schedule 5.

Subsection (3) states that Schedule 6 to the Act makes provision for financial relief in connection with civil partnerships that corresponds to provision made for financial relief in connection with marriages by the Domestic Proceedings and Magistrates Court Act 1978 (c.22).

Subsection (4) Schedule 7 to the Act makes provision for financial relief in England and Wales after a civil partnership has been dissolved or annulled, or civil partners have been legally separated, in a country outside the British Islands.

In the next chapter, we look at Civil Partnership Agreements and their contractual nature.

****

Chapter 6.

Civil Partnership Agreements

___

Civil partnership agreements unenforceable

Section 73 of the Civil Partnerships Act deals with civil partnership agreements and their contractual and other nature.

Subsection (1) of section 73 states that a civil partnership agreement does not under the law of England and Wales have effect as a contract giving rise to legal rights.

Subsection (2) states that no action lies in England and Wales for breach of a civil partnership agreement, whatever the law applicable to the agreement.

Subsection (2) states that in this section and section 74 (below) 'civil partnership agreement' means an agreement between two people:

a)   To register as civil partners of each other-

(i)   in England and Wales (under this part),

(ii)   in Scotland (in Part 3),

(iii)   in Northern Ireland (under Part 4), or

(iv)   outside the United Kingdom under an order in Council made under chapter 1 of Part 5 (registration at British Consulates etc, or by armed forces personnel) or

(v)   to enter into an overseas relationship.

Subsection (4) states that this section applies in relation to civil partnership agreements whether entered into before or after this section comes into force, but does not affect any action commenced before it comes into force.

Property where civil partnership agreement is terminated

Subsection (1) of section 74 states that section 74 applies if a civil partnership agreement is terminated. Subsection (2) states that section 65 (contributions by civil partners to property improvements) applies, in relation to any property in which either or both of the parties to the agreement had a beneficial interest while the agreement was in force, as it applies in relation to property in which a civil partner has a beneficial interest.

Subsection (3) states that sections 66 and 67 (disputes between civil partners about property) apply to any dispute between or claim by one of the parties in relation to property in which either or both had a beneficial interest while the agreement was in force, as if the parties were civil partners of each other.

Subsection (4) states that an application made under section 66 or 67 by virtue of subsection (3) must be made within 3 years of the termination of the agreement.

Subsection (5) states that a party to a civil partnership agreement who makes a gift of property to the other party on

112

the condition (express or implied) that it is to be returned if the agreement is terminated is not prevented from recovering the property merely because of his having terminated the agreement.

****

Chapter 7.

Civil Partnerships and Children

Children, Parental responsibility, children of the family and relatives

The welfare of children generally is of the utmost importance and Section 75 of the Civil Partnerships Act 2004 deals with the responsibility of civil partners to children and family following a civil partnership.

Subsection (1) of section 75 states that the Children's Act 1989 (c.41) (the 1989 Act) is amended as follows.

Subsection (2) defines the amendment, in section 4A(1)(acquisition of parental responsibility by stepparent after 'is married to' insert 'or a civil partner of'.

Subsection (3) states in section 105(1) (interpretation) for the definition of 'child of the family' (in relation to the parties to a marriage) substitute-

"child of the family", in relation to parties to a marriage, or two people who are civil partners of each other, means-

a) a child of both of them, and

b) any other child, other than a child placed with them as foster parents by a local authority or voluntary organisation, who has been treated by both of them as a child of their family".

Subsection (4) states that in the definition of "relative" in section 105(1), for "by affinity" substitute "by marriage or civil partnership".

Guardianship

Section 76 of the Act deals with guardianship of children. In section 6 of the 1989 Act (guardians: revocation and disclaimer) after subsection 3(A) insert-

"(3B) An appointment under section 5(3) or (4) (including one made in an unrevoked will or codicil) is revoked if the person appointed is the civil partner of the person who made the appointment and either-

a) an order of the court of civil jurisdiction in England and Wales dissolves or annuls the civil partnership, or

b) the civil partnership is dissolved or annulled and the dissolution or annulment is entitled to recognition in England and Wales by virtue of Chapter 3 of Part 5 of the Civil partnership Act 2004, unless a contrary intention appears by appointment.

Entitlement to apply for residence or contact order

Section 77 of the Act deals with entitlement to apply for residence or contact order. In section 10(5) of the 1989 Act (persons entitled to apply for residence or contact order) after paragraph (a) insert-" (as) any civil partner in a civil partnership (whether or not subsisting) in relation to whom the child is a child of the family".

Financial provision for children

Section 78 of the Act deals with financial provision for children. Subsection (1) of section 78 amends Schedule 1 to the 1989 Act (financial provision for children) as follows in subsection (2).

In paragraph 2(6) (meaning of periodical payments order) after paragraph (d) insert-

" (e) Part 1 or 9 of Schedule 5 to the Civil partnership Act 2004 (financial relief in the High Court or a county court etc);

(f) Schedule 6 to the 2004 Act (financial relief in the magistrate's court etc),".

Subsection (3) states that in paragraph 15(2) (person with whom a child lives or is to live) after "husband or wife" insert "or civil partner".

Subsection (4) states for paragraph 16(2) (extended meaning of "parent") substitute-

"(2) In this Schedule, except paragraphs 2 and 15, "parent" includes-

a) any party to a marriage (whether or not subsisting) in relation to whom the child concerned is a child of the family, and

b) any civil partner in a civil partnership (whether or not subsisting) in relation to whom the child concerned is a child of the family;

and for this purpose any reference to either parent or both parents shall be read as a reference to any parent of his and to all of his parents".

Adoption

Section 79 of the Act deals with civil partnership and adoption. Subsection (1) amends the Adoption and Children Act of 2002 (c.38) as follow.

Subsection (2) states in section 21 (placement orders) in subsection (4)(c) after "child marries" insert "forms a civil partnership".

Subsection (3) states in section 47 (condition for making adoption orders) after subsection (8) insert-

"(8A) An adoption order may not be made in relation to a person who is or has been a civil partner".

Subsection (4) states in section 51 (adoption by one person), in subsection (1) after " is not married" insert "or a civil partner".

Subsection (5) states after section 51(3) insert-

"(3A) An adoption order may be made on the application of one person who has attained the age of 21 years and is a civil partner if the court is satisfied that-

a) the persons civil partner cannot be found

b) the civil partners have separated and are living apart, and the separation is likely to be permanent, or

c) the persons civil partner is by reason of ill health, whether physical or mental, incapable of making an application for an adoption order".

Subsection (6) states in section 64 (other provisions to be made by regulations) in subsection (5) for "or marriage" substitute "marriage or civil partnership".

Subsection (7) states in section 74(1) (enactments for whose purposes section 67 does not apply) for paragraph (a) substitute-

"(a) section 1 of and Schedule 1 to the Marriage Act 1949 or Schedule 1 to the Civil Partnership Act 2004 (prohibited degrees of kindred and affinity).

Subsection (8) states in section 79 (connections between the register and birth records) , in subsection (7)-

a) in paragraph (b) after "intends to be married" insert "or forms a civil partnership" and

b) for "the person whom the applicant intends to marry" substitute "the intended spouse or civil partner".

119

Subsection (9) states in section 81 (Adoption Contact Register: supplementary), in subsection (2) for "or marriage" substitute marriage or civil partnership".

Subsection (10) states in section 98 (pre-commencement adoptions: information), in subsection (7), in the definition of "relative" for "or marriage" substitute "marriage or civil partnership".

Subsection (11) states in section 144 (interpretation), in the definition of "relative" in subsection (1), after "by marriage" insert "or civil partnership".

Subsection (12) states in section 144(4) (meaning of "couple"), after paragraph (a) insert-"(aa) two people who are civil partners of each other.

****

Chapter 8.

Civil Partnerships Formed or Dissolved Abroad

Registration outside U.K. under Order in Council.

Registration at British Consulates etc.

Section 210 of the CPA 2004 deals with registration at British Consulates and other matters.

Subsection (1) of section 210 states that Her Majesty may by Order in Council make provision for two people to register as civil partners of each other:

a) in prescribed countries or territories outside the United Kingdom, and

b) in the presence of a prescribed officer of Her Majesty's Diplomatic Service

.

in cases where the officer is satisfied that the conditions in subsection (2) below are met.

Subsection (2) lays out those conditions as follows:

a) at least one of the proposed civil partners is a United Kingdom national,

b) the proposed civil partners would have been eligible to register as civil partners of each other in such part of the United Kingdom as is determined in accordance with the order,

c) the authorities of the countries or territory in which it is proposed that they register as civil partners will not object to the registration, and

d) insufficient facilities exist for them to enter into an overseas relationship under the law of that country or territory.

Subsection (3) states that an officer is not required to allow two people to register as civil partners of each other if in his opinion the formation of a civil partnership between them would be inconsistent with international law or the comity of nations.

Subsection (4) states that an Order in Council under this section may make provision for appeals against a refusal, in reliance on subsection (3), to allow two people to register as civil partners of each other.

Subsection (5) states that an Order in Council under this section may provide that two people who register as civil partners of each other under such an order are to be treated for the purposes of sections 221(1)(c)(i) and(2)(c)(i),222©,224(b),225(c)(i) and (3)(c)(i),229(c)(i) and (2)(c)(i),230(c) and 232(b)(i) of the Presumption of Death (Scotland) Act 1977 (c.27) as if they had done so in the part of the United Kingdom determined as mentioned in subsection (2)(b).

Registration by armed forces personnel

Section 211 of the Act deals with armed forces personnel. Subsection (1) of section 211 states that her majesty may by Order in Council make provision for two people to register as civil partners of each other:

a) in prescribed countries or territories outside the United Kingdom, and

b) in the presence of an officer appointed by virtue of the Registration of Births, Deaths and marriages (Special Provisions) Act 1957 (c.58).

in cases where the officer is satisfied that the conditions in subsection (2) below are met. Subsection (2) lays out those conditions:

a) at least one of the proposed civil partners-

(i)   is a member of a part of Her Majesty's forces serving in the country or territory,

(ii)   is employed in the country or territory in such other capacity as may be prescribed, or

(iii)   is a child of a person falling within sub-paragraph (i) or (ii) and has his home with that person in that country or territory,

(b) the proposed civil partners would have been eligible to register as civil partners of each other in such part of the United Kingdom as is determined in accordance with the Order, and

(c) such other requirements as may be prescribed are complied with.

Subsection (3) states that in determining for the purposes of sub-section (2) whether one person is the child of another, a person who is or was treated by another as a child of the family in relation to:

a) a marriage to which the other is or was a party, or
b) a civil partnership in which the other is or was a civil partner

is to be regarded as the other's child.

Subsection (4) states that an Order in Council under this section may provide that two people who register as civil partners of each other under such an order are to be treated for the purposes of section 221(1)(c)(i) and (2)(c)(i),222 (c), 224(b) 225(1) (c) (i) 229(1)(c) (i) and (2) (c) (i) 230 (c) and 232 (b) and section 1 (3)(c)(i) of the Presumption of Death (Scotland) Act 1977 (c.27) as if they had done so in the part of the United Kingdom determined in accordance with subsection (2)(b).

Subsection 5 states that any references made in this section:
a) to a country or territory outside the United Kingdom,

b) to forces serving in such a country or territory, and

c) to persons employed in such a country or territory,

include references to ships which are for the time being in the waters of a country or territory outside the United Kingdom, to forces serving in any such ship and to persons employed in any such ship.

****

Chapter 9.

Overseas Relationships Treated as Civil Partnerships

Meaning of overseas relationship

Section 212 of the Act deals further with overseas relationships. Subsection (1) states that for the purposes of this Act an overseas relationship is a relationship which:

a) is either a specified relationship or a relationship which meets the general conditions, and

b) is registered (whether before or after the passing of this Act) with a responsible authority in a country or territory outside the United Kingdom, by two people-

   (i)   who under the relevant law are of the same sex at the time when they do so, and

   (ii) neither of whom is already a civil partner or lawfully married.

Subsection (2) states that in this chapter, "the relevant law" means the law of the country or territory where the relationship is registered (including its rules of private international law).

Specified relationships

Section 213 subsection (1) deals with specified relationships, as defined by Schedule 20 to the Act. Subsection (2) states that the Secretary of State may by an order amend Schedule 20 by:

a) adding a relationship,

b) amending the description of a relationship, and

c) omitting a relationship.

Subsection (3) states that no order may be made under this section without the consent of the Scottish Ministers and the Department of Finance and Personnel.

Subsection (4) states that the power to make an order under this section is excercisable by statutory instrument.

Subsection (5) states that an order which contains any provision (whether alone or with other provisions) amending Schedule 20 by-

a) amending the description of a relationship, or

b) omitting a relationship,

may not be made unless a draft of the statutory instrument containing the order is laid before, and approved by a resolution of, each house of parliament.

The general conditions

Section 214 deals with general conditions and civil partnerships abroad. The general conditions are that, under the relevant law:

- the relationship may not be entered into if either of the parties is already a party to a relationship of that kind or lawfully married,

a) the relationship is of an indeterminate duration, and

b) the effect of entering into it is that the parties are-

    (i)   treated as a couple either generally or for specified purposes, or

    (ii)   treated as married.

Overseas relationships treated as civil partnerships: the general rule

Section 215 deals with overseas relationships which are treated as civil partnerships. Subsection (10 states that two people are to be treated as having formed a civil partnership as a result of having registered an overseas relationship if, under the relevant law, they:

a) had capacity to enter into the relationship, and

b) met all requirements necessary to ensure the formal validity of the relationship.

Subsection (2) states that subject to subsection (3) below, the time when they are to be treated as having formed the civil partnership is the time when the overseas relationship is registered (under the relevant law) as having been entered into.

Subsection (3) states that if the overseas relationship is registered (under the relevant law) as having been entered into before this section comes into force, the time when they are treated as having formed a civil partnership is the time when this section comes into force.

Subsection (4) states that if:

a) before this section comes into force, a dissolution or annulment of the overseas relationship was obtained outside the United Kingdom, and

b) the dissolution or annulment would be recognised under Chapter 3 if the overseas relationship had been treated as a civil partnership at the time of the dissolution or annulment,

subsection (3) does not apply and subsections (1) and (2) have effect subject to subsection (5).

Subsection (5) states that the overseas relationship is not to be treated as having been a civil partnership for the purposes of any provisions except:

a) Schedules 7, 11 and 17 (financial relief in United Kingdom after dissolution or annulment obtained outside the United Kingdom);

b) Such provisions as are specified (with or without modifications) in an order under s 259;

c) Chapter 3 (so far as necessary for the purposes of paragraphs (a) and (b)).

Subsection (6) that this section is subject to sections 216, 217 and 218.

The same sex requirement

Section 216 deals with the same sex requirement. Subsection (1) states that two people are not to be treated as having formed a civil partnership as a result of having registered an overseas relationship if, at the critical time, they were not of the same sex under United Kingdom law.

Subsection (2) states that if a full gender recognition certificate is issued under the 2004 Act to a person who has registered an overseas relationship which is within subsection (4) below after the issue of the certificate the relationship is no longer prevented from being treated as a civil partnership on the ground that, at the critical time, the parties were not of the same sex.

Subsection (3) states that, however, subsection (2) does not apply to an overseas relationship which is within subsection (4) below if either of the parties has formed a subsequent civil partnership or lawful marriage.

Subsection (4) states that an overseas relationship is within this section if (and only if) at the time mentioned in section 215(2)-

a) one of the parties ("A") was regarded under the relevant law as having changed gender (but was not regarded under United Kingdom law as having done so), and
b) the other party was (under United Kingdom law) of the gender to which A had changed under the relevant law.

Subsection (5) states that, in this section-

"the critical time" means the time determined in accordance with section 215(2) or (as the case may be) (3);

"the 2004 Act" means the Gender Recognition Act 2004 (c.7);

"United Kingdom law" means any enactment or rule of law applying in England and Wales, Scotland and Northern Ireland.

Subsection (6) states that nothing in this section prevents the exercise of any enforceable community right.

Persons domiciled in a part of the United Kingdom

Section 217 deals with domicile in a part of the United Kingdom. Subsection 1 (2) of section 217 applies if an overseas relationship has been registered by a person who was at the time mentioned in section 215 (2) domiciled in England and Wales.

Subsection (2) states that the two people concerned are not to be treated as having formed a civil partnership if, at the time mentioned in section 215 (2)-

a) either of them was under 16, or

b) they would have been within prohibited degrees of relationship under Part 1 of schedule 1 if they had been registering as civil partners of each other in England and Wales.

Subsection (3) states that subsection (4) applies if an overseas relationship has been registered by a person who at the time mentioned in section 215 (2) was domiciled in Scotland.

Subsection (4) states that the two people concerned are not to be treated as having formed a civil partnership if, at the time mentioned in section 215 (2), they were not eligible by virtue of paragraph (b), (c) or (e) of section 86(1) to register in Scotland as civil partners of each other.

Subsection (5) states that subsection (6) applies if an overseas relationship has been registered by a person who at the time mentioned in section 215(2) was domiciled in Northern Ireland.

Subsection (6) states that the two people concerned are not to be treated as having formed a civil partnership if, at the time mentioned in s125 (2)-00

a) either of them was under 16,or

b) they would have been within prohibited degrees of relationship under Schedule 12 if they had been registering as civil partners of each other in Northern Ireland.

The public policy exception

Section 218 states that two people are not to be treated as having formed a civil partnership as a result of having entered into an overseas relationship if it would be manifestly contrary to public policy to recognise the capacity under the relevant law, of one or both of them to enter into the relationship.

****

PART THREE: SAME SEX MARRIAGES IN THE UK

Chapter 10.

The Marriage (Same Sex Couples) Act 2013

Following on from the introduction of the Civil Partnerships Act 2004, the introduction of the Marriage (Same Sex Couples) Act 2013 has introduced the right of marriage and religious ceremony for same sex couples. In Scotland The Marriage and Civil Partnership (Scotland) Act 2014 received Royal Assent on 12 March 2014. The first ceremonies took place on 31 December 2014. In Northern Ireland same Sex marriages became law on 13th January 2020 with the first ceremony taking place on 11th February 2020.

The following chapters outline the 2013 Act and the rights it confers on same sex couples.

The main provisions of the Marriage (Same Sex Couples) Act 2013 are:

1.To allow same sex couples to marry in a civil ceremony;

2. To allow same sex couples to marry in a religious ceremony where the religious organisation has "opted in"

3. To enable civil partners to convert their civil partnership into a marriage;

4. To enable married individuals to change their legal gender without having to end their marriage.

Marriage of same sex couples

Those couples not in an existing legal relationship were be able to give notice of marriage from **Thursday 13th March 2014**. The first marriage for same sex couples could therefore take place from Saturday 29th March 2014. This did not apply to a couple who were currently in a civil partnership.

Background

Under the previous law, a marriage could only be between a man and a woman. Marriage law in England and Wales is based on where the marriage ceremony takes place. The Marriage Act 1949 (the "Marriage Act") sets out that a marriage can be solemnized (solemnization is the legal ceremony which gives effect to the marriage) either in religious buildings, through a religious ceremony, or on secular (non-religious) premises, through a civil ceremony. The law makes particular provision relating to marriage according to the rites and ceremonies of the Church of England and the Church in Wales, and to marriages according to the rites and usages of the Jewish religion and the Quakers (Society of Friends).

As we have seen in the previous chapters, same sex couples may register a civil partnership under the Civil Partnership Act 2004 (the "Civil Partnership Act"). A civil partnership is only available to same sex couples and can only be conducted through a civil ceremony, although following legislative change in 2011 this may be held in a religious building subject to local authority approval of premises and the approval of the organisation itself.

Church of England

The position of the Church of England is different from that of other religious organisations for three main reasons:

- as the established Church, its Canons (church laws) form part of the law of the land;
- as the established Church, it can amend or repeal primary legislation through a Measure passed by its Synod, provided the Measure is subsequently approved by both Houses of Parliament and receives Royal Assent;
- its clergy are under a common law duty to marry a parishioner in his or her parish church. The Church in Wales has a similar duty by virtue of it previously being established (it became disestablished in 1920).

Summary of the Act

The main purpose of the Act is to enable same sex couples to marry, either in a civil ceremony (i.e. a civil ceremony in a register office or approved premises e.g. a hotel) or, provided that the religious organisation concerned is in agreement, on religious premises, with the marriage being solemnized through a religious ceremony. Key elements of the Act:

- provide that same sex couples can get married in England and Wales

- provide that such marriages are the same as marriages between a man and a woman under the law of England and Wales;

- permit marriage of same sex couples by way of a civil ceremony;

- permit marriage of same sex couples according to religious rites and usages where a religious organisation has opted in to that process (with the exception of the Church of England and the Church in Wales);

- provide a process by which the Church in Wales can request and obtain legislative change to allow marriages of same sex couples according to its rites if it wishes to do so;

- provide that there will be no obligation or compulsion on religious organisations or individuals to carry out or participate in a religious marriage ceremony of a same sex couple;

- provide protection under equality law for religious organisations and individuals who do not wish to marry same sex couples in a religious ceremony;

provide for reviews of:

- whether an order should be made permitting belief organisations to solemnize marriages and to consider what provision should be made in the order;

- the operation and future of the Civil Partnership Act in England and Wales;

- survivor benefits under occupational pension schemes.

The Act does not remove the availability of civil partnerships for same sex couples. There is provision in the Act for those in a civil partnership to convert that relationship to a marriage if they choose to do so.

Religious organisations and their representatives who do not wish to marry same sex couples are protected from being compelled to do so through a series of religious protections, including:

- an explicit provision in the Act that no religious organisation can be compelled to opt in to marry same sex couples or to permit this to happen in their place of worship, and no religious organisation or individual can be compelled to conduct religious same sex marriage ceremonies;

- amendments which the Act makes to the Equality Act 2010, to provide that it is not unlawful discrimination for a religious organisation or individual to refuse to marry a same sex couple in a religious ceremony;

- an "opt-in" mechanism whereby a marriage of a same sex couple cannot be carried out on religious premises or with a religious ceremony without the express consent of the religious organisation's governing body;

- ensuring that the Act does not interfere with Anglican Canon law or ecclesiastical law;

- ensuring that the common law duty on Church of England and Church in Wales clergy to marry parishioners does not extend to same sex couples.

The Act does not amend marriage legislation to allow Church of England clergy to solemnize marriage of same sex couples according to its rites, and specific provision is made to ensure that the nature of marriage in Anglican Canon law is unaltered. Specific provision is made to ensure that the common law duty to marry parishioners, which applies to the clergy of both the Church of England and the Church in Wales, (and any corresponding right of parishioners to be married by such clergy) does not extend to same sex couples. In order to be able to solemnize marriages of same sex couples, therefore, the Church of England would have to put a Measure before Parliament amending the law to allow this to happen. The Church in Wales is unable to do this, and so the Act provides a power by which this must be done by the Lord Chancellor, by order, should the Governing Body of the Church in Wales request it.

The Act also contains a number of other related provisions, including provisions that enable a person to change their legal gender without ending their existing marriage; provisions dealing with consular marriage and marriage on armed forces bases overseas; and recognition of certain marriages of same sex couples formed outside England and Wales. There are also consequential and interpretative provisions clarifying how the

142

new law will affect a number of matters, such as state and occupational pensions.

A number of the provisions of the Act are to be given effect through subordinate legislation. Further details of these delegated powers are included in the Delegated Powers Memorandum and explained in the commentary on sections and schedules below.

Overview of the structure of the Act

The Act is largely an amending Act, making amendments to various pieces of primary legislation including:

- the Marriage Act 1949,
- the Equality Act 2010,
- the Marriage (Registrar General's Licence) Act 1970,
- the Matrimonial Causes Act 1973,
- the Domicile and Matrimonial Proceedings Act 1973,
- the Social Security Contributions and Benefits Act 1992,
- the Pension Schemes Act 1993,
- the Civil Partnership Act 2004,
- the Gender Recognition Act 2004.

The Act consists of 21 sections and 7 schedules arranged as follows:

Part 1 (sections 1-11) (Marriage of same sex couples in England and Wales) contains the main provisions of the Act relating to marriage of same sex couples and Schedules 1 to 4 contain consequential and interpretative provisions relating to Part 1.

Part 2 (sections 12-16) (Other provisions relating to marriage and civil partnership) deal with the change of legal gender of a married person or civil partner and marriage overseas (as do Schedules 5 and 6) and with the reviews of marriage by belief organisations, of the operation and future of the Civil Partnership Act in England and Wales and of survivor benefits under occupational pension schemes.

Part 3 (sections 17-21) (Final provisions) and Schedule 7 contain the standard technical provisions of the Act, including order-making powers and procedures, interpretation, extent and commencement.

Territorial extent and application

General

The territorial extent and application of the Act is England and Wales only, except for particular provisions as follows:

Provisions which extend to Scotland

In Part 1 of the Act, section 10(3), which gives effect to Schedule 2. Schedule 2 deals with the treatment in the rest of the United Kingdom of marriages of same sex couples under the law of England and Wales.

Scotland

17.The Act provides for marriage of same sex couples to be lawful in England and Wales only. However, as we have seen The Marriage and Civil Partnership (Scotland) Act 2014 received Royal Assent on 12 March 2014. The first ceremonies took place on 31 December 2014.

Wales

The Act allows for marriage of same sex couples in Wales, where the effect will be the same as that in England. Marriage of same sex couples will be equivalent to marriage of opposite sex couples except in certain cases. Existing legislation will be understood as applying to same sex couples as it has done until now to opposite sex couples. New legislation will be read as applying in the same way to same sex couples as to opposite sex couples.

As explained above, the Act does not permit religious marriage ceremonies in accordance with the rites of the Church in Wales. However, it does contain provision for the Church in Wales to request a change in the law to enable the marriage of same sex couples according to the rites of the Church in Wales, should it wish to do so (see section 8 of the Act).

Northern Ireland

Marriage is an area which is a devolved matter for Northern Ireland. The Act does not affect Northern Ireland directly, except as follows:

- there are amendments to the law in Northern Ireland as it relates to re-issuing and correcting errors in gender recognition certificates and fraud proceedings under the Gender Recognition Act 2004;

- the Act provides that marriages of same sex couples under the law of England and Wales will be treated as civil partnerships under the law of Northern Ireland.

The UK Government has proceeded in accordance with the convention that the UK Parliament does not normally legislate with regard to devolved matters in Northern Ireland except with the agreement of the Northern Ireland legislature. There are a number of provisions within the Act which triggered the convention. In addition to the provision of the Act which affects Northern Ireland directly (the treatment of same sex couples married in England and Wales), another provision which triggered that convention is a power for the Secretary of State to make consequential amendments in devolved areas. Other similar provisions include those which relate to the change of legal gender of married persons or civil partners. Any orders or regulations made under the Act which make provision that would otherwise be within the legislative competence of the Northern Ireland Assembly will require the consent of the Department of Finance and Personnel. Section 13 of the Act repeals the Foreign Marriage Act 1892, and Schedule 6 provides for a new regime of consular marriages and marriages on armed forces bases overseas in respect of both opposite sex and same

146

sex couples. The Northern Ireland Assembly made a decision not to include section 13 of, or Schedule 6 to, the Act in the Legislative Consent Motion it passed on 24 June 2013. As a result, the Act excludes Northern Ireland from the new provisions regarding consular marriage and marriage on armed forces bases overseas.

****

Further information

Equality unit https://www.gov.uk/society-and-culture/equality

Stonewall can provide information on www.stonewall.org.uk

Northern Ireland information on civil partnerships and same sex marriages go to www.nidirect.gov.uk

For information on civil partnerships and same sex marriages in **Scotland go** to www.nrscotland.gov.uk

Tax-contact your local tax office or go to www.hmrc.gov.uk

Pensions-contact the pension service on 0800 731 7898
https://www.gov.uk/contact-pension-service

Social security benefits-contact the benefit enquiry line on 0800 169 0314

Tax credits contact the Tax Credits help line on 0345 300 3900

Child Benefit- contact the Child Benefit Help line on 0300 200 3103

Child Support agency- contact 0845 713 3133

Adoption-Helpline   Adoption   UK   0300   666   0006
www.adoptionuk.org/one-one-support/helpline

Immigration-contact the immigration and Nationality Directorate www.gov.uk/government/organisations/uk-visas-and-immigration

Relationship support – contact relate on 0300 003 0396 www.relate.org.uk

Domestic Violence – 0808 2000 247   24 hour Freephone www.nationaldomesticviolencehelpline.org.uk

****

INDEX

****

Emerald Guides

www.straightforwardco.co.uk

Titles in the Emerald Series:

Law

Guide to Bankruptcy

Conducting Your Own Court case

Guide to Consumer law

Creating a Will

Guide to Family Law

Guide to Employment Law

Guide to European Union Law

Guide to Health and Safety Law

Guide to Criminal Law

Guide to Landlord and Tenant Law

Guide to the English Legal System

Guide to Housing Law

Guide to Marriage and Divorce

Guide to The Civil Partnerships Act

Guide to The Law of Contract

The Path to Justice

You and Your Legal Rights

Powers of Attorney

Managing Divorce and Separation

Health

Guide to Combating Child Obesity

Asthma Begins at Home

Alternative Health and Alternative Remedies

Explaining Arthritis

Music

How to Survive and Succeed in the Music Industry

General

A Practical Guide to Obtaining probate

A Practical Guide to Residential Conveyancing

Writing The Perfect CV

Keeping Books and Accounts-A Small Business Guide

Business Start Up-A Guide for New Business

Finding Asperger Syndrome in the Family-A Book of Answers

Explaining Autism Spectrum Disorder

Explaining Alzheimers

Explaining Parkinsons

Writing True Crime

Becoming a Professional Writer

Writing your Autobiography

For details of the above titles published in the Emerald Guides Series go to:

www.straightforwardco.co.uk